TEACHING AND MORALITY

TEACHING AND MORALITY

FRANCIS C. WADE, S.J.

Marquette University

LOYOLA UNIVERSITY PRESS *Chicago*

1963

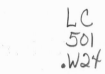

FOR REVEREND GERARD SMITH, S.J.
Teacher, whose wisdom
lives within his love of God

ACKNOWLEDGMENTS

The author owes a public debt of gratitude to many persons. Some he cannot even name now, because their borrowed ideas took root in his mind so thoroughly that they now appear native to the soil. Some persons have been named in the footnotes as authors whose books were consulted in preparing the manuscript. Four others, in neither category, have a right to special mention. Professor David R. Host, of the Marquette University School of Journalism, read the manuscript in its early stages and insisted on the kind of detailed clarity philosophers forget when speaking to other philosophers. Father Thomas E. Davitt, S.J., a colleague in the Philosophy Department, suggested at just the right moment the advantage of looking at students' assents when considering teaching. Father Charles W. Mulligan, S.J., edited the manuscript with the kind of knowledgeable competence that makes the author a better writer than he is. Finally, Miss Esther H. Diehl, former secretary to the Philosophy Department, prepared the manuscript with such loving care and sustained enthusiasm that the author was shamed into finishing the book.

CONTENTS

TEACHING AND MORALITY

CHAPTER 1

THE PROBLEM

This book deals with the relation of teaching to moral virtue in a Catholic liberal arts college. In its simplest terms,
the issue can be stated in this way: Do such colleges propose to make their students knowing or good or both

knowing and good? This question would seem to have only one answer: to make their students both knowing and good. But once this answer is given questions arise. Knowledge can be taught; virtue cannot. Thus no question arises regarding knowledge, since teaching deals with knowledge and colleges above all teach. The question arises regarding moral virtue, which cannot be taught. Colleges propose to teach students. Since they cannot teach virtue, what do they propose to do about the virtue of their students?

An easy answer is, "Nothing." But such an answer is only easy; it is not acceptable. Two reasons exclude it as an answer. First, no social action can prescind from morality, not even in the abstract. In teaching, one person helps another. And help that does not include moral improvement at least implicitly is not the kind of helping society can permit. Secondly, a college is a social institution intended to perfect the young. If knowledge is not sufficiently perfective unless it is accompanied by moral virtue, then a college cannot be uninterested in the virtue of its students. We shall establish this point in Chapter 2. Here we make it quickly by a series of questions. Could you conduct a college with a student body composed entirely of the vicious? If you could, would you be justified in making the vicious more learned? And what justification is there for making them more learned unless it is that they give up their vices, or at least be distracted by the worthwhile?

It seems that colleges may not be uninterested in moral virtue; at the same time they cannot teach virtue. Hence the question of what colleges propose to do about the virtue of their students.

When we limit our consideration to college teaching, the subject of this book is clearly part of a larger one, the relation of teaching to moral virtue. And behind that subject is the basic one, the relation of knowledge to virtue. If one thinks that knowledge is virtue, he will see no problem in teaching virtue. If one thinks that virtue is knowledge (likely to be called "wisdom"), he will have no problem. But all who think that knowledge is not virtue and virtue not knowledge—that is, a man can be learned and bad, or ignorant and good—will have a problem. And one that must be faced at least in the practical order where students are being taught in schools that open their doors daily. Should schools in fact give primacy to knowledge or primacy to moral virtue?

The tension between these two ends of schooling has always been operative in Western higher education, though not always in the same form. Ancient Greece had advocates of both positions. The Platonic tradition emphasized speculative knowledge as the crown of education. Isocrates emphasized practical knowledge, that of the orator who could deal prudently with moral, human reality.[1] In Roman higher education the opposition was not between speculative and practical knowledge but between a practical knowledge of the noble orator who could make good moral judgments and a practical knowledge that was purely utilitarian techniques of rhetoric. Cicero, and Quintilian after him, were not listened to when they defended the former position, that the ideal of education was the noble orator.[2] In thirteenth-century Europe, the two most influential bodies of university teachers were the Franciscans, led by St. Bonaventure, and the Dominicans, led by St. Thomas Aquinas. The Franciscans tended to emphasize the good, the Dominicans the true, in their teaching of theology.[3]

In the United States today the tension is between adjustment (or one of its variants) and intellectual excellence. That morality is not formally one of the poles of tension is not surprising in a pluralist society that demands no universal agreement on what morality is or what is moral. What produces the tension here is rather the democratic ideal of education for all. Since all are not able to achieve intellectual excellence, there must be an ideal that is generally achievable. Most can adjust to be good citizens. Notice the parallel with the moral, which is what all men are bound to, and the intellectual, which men may or may not achieve and still be good men. The close connection between the ideal of adjustment and moral virtue can be seen in Catholic schools. Here there is agreement about what morality is and what is moral. Here, also, "adjustment" turns out to be acquiring the moral (and supernatural) virtues. Consequently, the contemporary educational problem as viewed specifically in a Catholic college is the tension between the ideals of knowledge and of moral virtue.

This viewpoint requires a double limitation to our subject. The teaching considered here is that in a Catholic liberal arts college. There are two reasons for limiting the present discussion to college teaching only. The first is personal, that the author has had experience in teaching in college, some twenty years of it. The second reason is the nature of the American college, whose adult students, some of them at least, pursue knowledge at a level where it could possibly be, or at least be thought by outsiders to be, either separated from moral virtue or independent of it. High schools generally do not face this precise issue. When morality enters the discussion of high-school education, it generally takes the form of disciplinary problems, not of

4

the relation of knowledge to virtue. Whatever the reason is, the fact is clear enough. Knowledge must reach a high level of excellence before it will compete for equal status with moral virtue. Only here does one have to relate the two quite precisely.

The reason for speaking specifically of a Catholic college is not itself a "Catholic" reason. That is, I do not propose a theological answer to our question; consequently, I shall not appeal to authority in any of its sources. The only appeal in these pages will be to reason made by reason, though by a reason that also has the faith. My purpose, therefore, in limiting our question is not a partisan one. Nor is it a purely personal one—that I have taught only in such colleges. My purpose is primarily to get the question of morality and teaching down to definite, describable situations where a clear answer can be given. The Catholic holds firmly that Christianity is revealed by God and that this revelation is made definite and precise by the Church teaching with authority. Such concrete religious commitments, generally made prior to teaching and being taught in college, influence the work of both teacher and student in a Catholic college. Here we have something definite and detailed for consideration. In these describable situations, how are knowledge and virtue related?

This limitation of our discussion by no means implies that it is in Catholic colleges only that the problem arises. The relation of knowledge to virtue is a problem for every Christian teacher or school. Actually, it is no less a problem for any teacher or school, private or public, though one that easily gets lost when adjustment takes the place of virtue or when men agree that value judgments are not the concern of teachers and schools. This last position, that teachers should take no sides concerning good and bad, is open to discussion.[4] It will not be discussed here except implicitly. Our topic is the relation of teaching to moral virtue in a Catholic liberal arts college.

The very importance of this problem in the practical order encourages one to find an answer quickly. Colleges are being run; something must be done about the moral virtue of students. The pressure of circumstances favors taking a position, even if one has not thought out very carefully what is at stake. One might, for instance, think that moral virtue is fostered by exhortation and that colleges should therefore insist on frequent moral exhortations in the classroom. This solution to our problem keeps a semblance of unity in the teacher's task. At least the same man in the same place does both jobs, even though the act of teaching is a different act from that of exhorting. Another person might think that all teaching should directly edify the student and that truths not patently edifying should be either excluded or minimized. This solution also keeps a semblance of unity. The same man, the teacher, does both, because he orders knowledge, at least negatively, as a means to virtue. A third person might think that the classroom should be reserved for teaching and that religious extracurricular societies, leagues, and so on, should be added to foster moral virtue. This solution boldly and completely separates learning and virtuous activity into two separate ends with separate means and possibly with separate agents, the teacher and the counselor or moderator.

This separation of teaching and exhorting (or counseling) has its advantages in some situations. Faced with a questionnaire on what the college does for the morality of its students, a college official, always busy putting out fires started by someone else, might be relieved to be able to list a number of such extracurricular activities. If his list seems too short, the problem is not very difficult; all he need do is detail someone to get more activities started. He might, by contrast, be embarrassed to have to put down: "Our teaching provides the major moral influence on the student." His embarrassment, I think, would be groundless. The conclusion of this book is that college teaching is saturated with factors that foster moral virtue. By college teaching I do not mean a mixture of teaching and exhortation or merely teaching edifying truths; I mean plain teaching students to know subjects taught them, whatever the subjects may be. Moreover, no position will be taken on the utility or futility of extracurricular activities, other than the negative one implied in the book's conclusion. That is, extracurricular activities are not the only, or the main, means a college has for fostering virtue; or putting it positively, a college precisely in its distinctive acts of teaching is a powerful influence to moral virtue.

The danger of the quick answers given above—classroom exhortation, edifying truths, extracurricular activities —is not that they have no justification. Certainly there is place for all three of them. Moreover, the very demands of the practical order may on occasion justify acting as if one or the other is the best answer here and now. One has to act and act today. Yet the demands of the practical order will not forever justify selling out to the kind of mediocrity that sacrifices a greater for a lesser good. This line of action, as a matter of fact, carries its own punishment with it. The punishment is not merely that men settle for mediocrity (occasionally we all have a Munich of our own); the punishment is that the very best efforts are predestined to mediocre results at best, mainly because no better is known. What is needed is better knowledge. This better knowledge will come from many minds facing the practical problem as sharply and as honestly as possible and trying to work out an answer that does justice to all the human factors involved.

Facing a practical problem sharply does not always mean finding new facts, or making old facts more definite, by processes generally designated as research. Sometimes it means understanding facts that are obvious enough to all by tracing their taproots into deeper soil. Knowledge of this soil may tell more about the branches above than any study of them would ever reveal. The soil of our present problem is the nature of teaching (and being taught) and the nature of moral choices. Misunderstanding about these actions will be an open invitation either to force teaching into attempting what it cannot do or to force nonteaching activities into doing poorly what teaching can do better. Looking closely at the nature of teaching and moral choices may reveal the fact that learning in a college is so saturated with moral factors that the very act of teaching can do for the moral life of the student what nothing else can do. That is the position this book is intended to establish.

Here is the order in which our topic will be discussed. First, some inadequate statements of this relation will be considered. The setting of this consideration will be that of the objectives of a Catholic college. Having pointed out the inadequacies of some proposed statements of the relation of teaching to moral virtue, we shall propose a solution based on the difference between knowledge and the state of its possession. In Chapter 3, this distinction is presented

8

and applied to teaching in college. Each of these factors in learning is considered separately in Chapters 4 and 5. In Chapter 6 we point out the results of neglecting either the knowledge factor in learning or the conditions of possession of the learned knowledge. In Chapter 7 we consider the relation of taught knowledge to actual moral choice. The final and summary chapter will formulate an answer to these questions: What does a Catholic liberal arts college, in its teaching, do for the moral virtue of the student? What are the objectives of a Catholic liberal arts college?

CHAPTER 2

SOME

INADEQUATE

SOLUTIONS

This chapter has both a negative and positive purpose. The negative purpose is to fill up some of the holes that men have dug around our question; the positive purpose is to level the ground for a safer path. The leveler used is a philosophical understanding of the role of the object of a power and the end of an action. But our present interest is not to examine the leveler, a task that requires much patience plus a taste for philosophical analysis. It is quite sufficient at present to smooth the ground by filling the holes. That is, some of the holes, enough, at least, to make a safe path possible. If our leveler does this reasonably, it will have justified itself indirectly and sufficiently.

Not all the solutions that men have proposed to our question of teaching and moral virtue are of equal significance. Some solutions considered in this chapter are shallow, some more profound; yet all of them are attractive, as I can testify from my own experience of subscribing to each of them at one time or another. Nevertheless, they are inadequate and serve to hide from view an answer better than they can provide. To make their inadequacies evident, we shall examine them singly, beginning with the shallow proposals first.

General solutions to our problem have their own attraction. Thus one can talk with a satisfying surety about "developing the whole man, naturally and supernaturally." As a statement of the objectives of a college this formulation is dead right. And in some practical situations it may be of great help for improving the work of a college. But in facing our present problem more is lost than gained by talking of "developing the whole man." The very generality of this statement invites one to ask: How is the whole man developed? Certainly the whole man, perfected naturally and supernaturally, must be developed intellectually and morally. And this brings us back to the problem of how a school proposes to develop moral virtues, which admittedly cannot be taught. Thus little is gained by talking of the "whole man." Rather, something has been lost; namely, the clear vision of where precisely the problem resides. Perhaps a given question cannot be answered. But this at least is certain, to cover a problem under a layer of generalities will not help much towards its solution.

There are other general approaches. Some, taking a page from psychoanalysis, think of education as life-adjustment. The objective of a college, they say, is the preparation of men to take their rightful place in this world and the next. Clearly this is a statement of the objective of a Catholic college. But, for the same reasons as noted above, it is too general to be of any great help in getting below the skin of the problem. Men lacking in moral virtue would hardly be prepared to take any human place either in this world or the next. In other words, the question remains whole and entire: How does a Catholic college produce, train in or educate to, develop, encourage or foster moral virtue?

Any general statement of the objectives of a Catholic college will be inadequate precisely because of its generality. To be specific and definite some clarifying concepts must be introduced. These concepts will serve to break open and distinguish the separate parts of the problem, as preparation, of course, to putting the factors together again into an intelligible whole. A number of such "clarifying" concepts will be presented. We shall test these for their adequacy. As we do so, respect will grow for those who have retreated into general statements of objectives, which have at least the merit of not saying more than was intended.

The first of these clarifying distinctions is that of "direct-indirect objectives." It would be applied to teaching in this way: The direct objective is knowledge; virtue would be

12

the indirect objective. To see what this means requires a closer look at the distinction.

The first meaning of *direct* is applied to actions involving local motion. A bird flying in a straight line would fly directly to a place; if it zigzagged, it would follow an indirect path. Not all actions, indeed, involve local motion. But all actions which begin and cease to be are like local actions in this, that they have a beginning point (agent), a transition period (action), and a point of arrival (end). Thus *direct* can be applied to other actions than local motion. But notice where the word most properly fits the data. Directness is a characteristic of the way the action attains the end. In spite of the fact that we speak of the direct end or objective, the end is not primarily direct. Its directness comes from the directness of the action attaining it. If one wishes to bypass the action and consider the end as determining the action, he would do better to talk about a primary and secondary end. Direct ends are direct only because the action achieving them is direct.

Direct action of the local sort will be on a straight line between beginning and end (stopping place). Direct action of the nonlocal sort will be one which intelligibly, rather than spatially, joins agent to end (effect). The straightness of such action consists in its power to account for the effect without bringing in any other action. Here is intelligible straightness: Singer (agent) sings (action) a song (effect produced). Between singer and song all that is needed is singing to join the two in the most intelligible way. But here there is no intelligible straightness: A singer (agent) sings (action) and makes the audience angry (effect). Singing will not join singer and angry audience; something else—say the haughtiness of the singer—must be added in order to make this connection intelligible. From these examples it is possible to see the factor that accounts for intelligible straightness. It is similarity between action and effect. Between singing and song there is similarity; between singing and angry audience there is no similarity and directness. A song is the direct effect of singing; an angry audience is the indirect effect of singing.

We have considered directness from the effect back to the action. It can be looked at from the front, and then effect becomes end or objective. Where there is a direct intelligible line of similarity between action and its end, this end is properly called the direct objective, for it is on the main intelligible line through agent-action-end. When something else, not on the main line but on a sideline, is achievable, this is called the indirect objective. For example, the manufacturer's action of making a salable garment issues directly in the salable garment, the direct objective. This same action may also issue in an advantage over his competitors, an indirect objective. Even though especially intended, advantage over his competitors is not in the direct line of the action of making a garment. There is no similarity between making a salable garment and having advantage over his competitors. He could have an advantage without making such a garment. He could make the garment and yet have no advantage over his competitors. In other words, the action and its direct objective are not separable; given one, you have the other. But action and its indirect objectives are separable, so that having one does not guarantee having the other. However—and this is important—when an action does attain its indirect object, it is really the cause of that object. In our example, the advantage over competitors, when attained by making a salable garment, is the result of making a salable garment. The difference between direct and indirect objectives is not this, that one is and one is not attained by some action. The difference rather is that one action attains both objectives but in different ways, one directly and the other indirectly.

Applied to our problem the distinction would be that a college's direct objective[1] in its teaching activity is knowledge in the student, and its indirect objective is moral virtue in the student. No matter how well this distinction helps us understand some aspect of teaching, it labors under two self-imposed handicaps here. The first is that knowledge is made the essential of the action of teaching; and this leaves moral virtue in the position of being nonessential. Yet common sense, backed by the experience of any conscientious teacher, seems to rebel at the notion that virtue is not an essential of the act of teaching. Even those who use this distinction by no means intend to play down the importance of moral virtue in the enterprise of teaching. For example, J. Maritain, after saying, "Neither intuition nor love is a matter of training and learning, they are gift and freedom. In spite of all that, education should be primarily concerned with them,"[2] goes on to say:

> Concerning *direct* action on the will and the shaping of character, this objective chiefly depends on educational spheres other than school and college education—not to speak of the role which the extra-educational sphere plays in this matter. On the contrary, concerning *indirect* action on the will and the character, school and college education provide a basic and necessary preparation for the main objective in question by concentrating on knowledge and the intellect, not on the will and direct moral training, and by keeping sight, above all, of the development and uprightness

of the speculative and practical reason. School and college education has indeed its own world, which essentially consists of the dignity and achievements of knowledge and the intellect, that is, of the human being's root faculty.[3]

The whole point of Maritain's distinction between direct and indirect action on the will is to guarantee to the act of teaching a special influence in developing moral rectitude, with which education is primarily concerned. Still, he ends by saying that schools and colleges essentially achieve knowledge, because teaching, their essential function, directly acts on the intellect and only indirectly acts on the will. And when this is said, even though true, the distinction leaves knowledge essential to teaching, and moral virtue becomes perforce nonessential. There seems to be no way to keep a dichotomy from dichotomizing.

The second handicap set up by the direct-indirect distinction is its implicit position about the cause of moral virtue. Once knowledge is granted as the direct objective, it is also taken for granted that moral virtue is the indirect objective of teaching. Recall what was said about the direct and indirect objective, that the distinction bears on the way the actions attain an end. The distinction is not this: One action is the cause of one end and not the cause of the other. In the example used above, the one action both caused the salable garment and caused the advantage over competitors, when such existed. But knowledge has never caused moral virtue, mainly because virtuous acts must be free and self-originated in order to be virtuous. However knowledge and virtue are related, neither seems to be the cause, direct or indirect, of the other.

Both of these handicaps—the implication that virtue is not essential to teaching and that teaching is the indirect cause of virtue—are not harmless inadequacies. They invite trouble. Both are invitations to introduce nonteaching activities into college life—God knows we have enough already. If teaching has no essential relation to moral virtue, it could be argued, educators had better get busy and find some activities that are essentially related to virtue. And the one who raises his voice to protect teaching and learning from a swarm of distracting activities finds himself jockeyed into the position of being against virtue. Yes or no, is there any essential relation between knowledge and virtue? Yes or no, is virtue essential to college education? He cannot refuse to answer; he cannot live with either his yes or his no. Again, if teaching only attains moral virtue indirectly, it is high time we found something that will attain it directly. Why should one stop to inquire if any school activity will cause moral virtue? One has been invited to think that such activities can cause virtue. Grant that teaching causes virtue indirectly. One must also grant that it can be caused directly by some action other than teaching. And to oppose multiplying such activities in a college will be laid to the perverseness of a proud intellectualism that is not satisfied until it remakes everything to its own image and likeness.

In short, the distinction between direct and indirect objectives has little to commend itself when applied to knowledge and virtue in schooling. Its strong point is its insistence on the primacy of knowledge in teaching. But this very insistence only strengthens the hand of those who oppose the primacy of knowledge. For it concedes to them alone the high quality of zeal for the moral virtue of the student and banishes the dedicated teacher to the doorstep of his own home.

The realization of the importance of moral virtue to the whole enterprise of teaching and running colleges leads to a second attempt at clarification. It consists in saying that a Catholic college has two equally direct ends, knowledge and moral virtue. The force of this position arises from two patent facts. First, knowledge is a good in itself, just as virtue is, so that a bad man can be learned and a good man unlearned. Second, it seems unsatisfactory either to relate knowledge and virtue as direct and indirect ends or to exclude either from the status of end of a Catholic college. One way out of this impasse is to try to keep both moral virtue and knowledge as ends; make both of them direct ends of the college and both equally direct ends. A train needs two rails and needs both equally. In this way virtue as the end of the college is just as important as knowledge.

The trouble with this way out is that it gets us out of the frying pan only to drop us into the fire. The frying pan that is intolerably hot is the position that virtue is not a direct end of a college. But it lands us in the hotter position that the college carries on two distinct lines of action, one ordered to knowledge and the other to moral virtue. One action, we know from metaphysics, can have only one direct end, since the end specifies the kind of action done. If, for example, the direct end is shoes made, then shoe-making actions are demanded; and any other action—say, writing—will never issue in shoes. Everyone, not only the metaphysician, knows quite well that the direct end specifies the action. Now, the problem is not that colleges have only one action, for patently, they do many things, from teaching aesthetics all the way to fielding a football team. The problem rather is whether there is one set of actions whose direct end is moral virtue and another set whose direct end is knowledge. Grant that the answer to this question is yes; that is, that both knowledge and virtue are equally direct ends and therefore equally important. Then it must be granted that the college ought to spend as much time and attention on training to virtue as it does on training to knowledge. This would mean that for every teaching period there would have to be an equivalent period of counseling (or retreat exercises, or sermons, or reception of sacraments). In fact, the equivalent time would hardly be adequate, since it is easier, where talent is roughly equal, to acquire knowledge than it is to acquire moral virtue. More time would have to be devoted to virtue than to knowledge. Colleges would thus be half novitiates and half teaching institutions, and possibly neither.

But the fire of this position is hotter than has so far been indicated. For knowledge and virtue cannot be equally important ends, not for a Catholic college. Catholics must believe as a matter of faith that man is saved not by the liberal arts and sciences but by grace-elevated acts of virtue. Moral virtue is therefore a necessary part of the end of man in a way that college-learned knowledge is not. Consequently, moral virtue must take supremacy wherever there is question of ordering virtue and knowledge. To see this point, consider the case of a brilliant student who is blatantly immoral. A college administrator, faced with such a student, does not say, "Well, there are two equally direct ends." He says, and rightly so, "Get out of school." That is, virtue becomes the controlling end of a school and knowledge takes second place. And what began as an attempt to save a place for virtue in the college ends up in undermining the place of knowledge. A strange problem, no doubt, to have to justify knowledge in schools, and one that would seem, at this late date in Western civilization, to be wholly unnecessary. Indeed, the fire is hotter than the frying pan.

Another way to state the position that both knowledge and virtue are the direct ends of education is to say that the proper end[4] of Christian education is Christian perfection; that is, a vigorous life of sanctifying grace.[5] The reasons for this position will be taken from sacred theology. Christian perfection, which consists essentially in the love of God, is the end of every Christian action. It is also the end of Christian education. No Christian can deny this. But he can say that the very universality of this end defeats its power to explain much about teaching. For if actions are specified by their proper and proximate ends, how can an end (Christian perfection) common to all actions specify any one kind of action without making all actions be specifically the same? Admit that the proper and proximate end determines the kind of action done. Then Christian perfection cannot be the proper and proximate end of teaching, taking a vacation, writing a book. These are different actions. Their proper ends must be different, even though they all are orderable to Christian perfection.[6]

However, there is another way of looking at education. Instead of focusing on the distinct actions involved, look rather at the achievement effected by these actions. We are encouraged to do so because educating and schooling are wholly preparatory actions. They are ordered to an achievable state, which is one. The state to be achieved is indeed the proper end of the educating actions. It may even be called the proximate end. But the meaning of *proximate* and *proper* has been shifted now. The shift is

owing to their reference to a state achieved by different
kinds of action rather than to the different actions that
achieved this state. For example, the state of being a
teacher has as its proximate and proper end to teach. It is
not, however, the proximate end of the teacher's own
learning. Learning is an immanent action, one that perfects the learner; teaching is a transient action, one that
perfects the student, not the teacher. Obviously they cannot, as actions, have the same proximate and proper ends.
But the state of being a teacher, which includes acquiring knowledge and the art of teaching, does have as its
proximate end the good of teaching. The same holds for
education. To say that the direct and proximate end of
Christian education is Christian perfection is eminently
true. Also, it supplies us with a norm for judging the result of schooling. It does not tell us much, though, about
the specifically different actions by which the result is
finally achieved.

There is one advantage, however, to this formulation of
the end of Christian education. It protects one from saying
more than he intended to say. There is always the temptation to identify education with teaching, its most characteristic action, and then to point out that teachers teach
knowledge. Next, one must add that virtue cannot be
taught. At this point one has to start looking around for
distinctions that will save a place for moral virtue in the
school, which is essentially or primarily or directly or properly or immediately ordered to knowledge. This last proposition about the role of knowledge in the school is, I think,
true. Also, it is inadequate. Its inadequacy is shown precisely by appealing to the state that should be the result of
Christian schooling. That state is not one in which moral

virtue is not essential and primary and proper. If both knowledge and virtue are essential, primary and proper, why pick out one (knowledge) for such pronounced emphasis? Still, the corrective value of the formula "The end of education is Christian perfection" does not exempt the formula itself from needing correction. As we indicated above, when virtue and knowledge compete for attention, virtue must win with all who hold that good choices make a man good, whereas good knowledge only makes a man knowing. At this point one will have to play down knowledge, at least where it seems to cross virtue. One will also have to say that novitiates are schools in the most precise sense of the word.[7] And having said this, even quietly to oneself, one should suspect the facts are draining from a hole in his formula.

There is a fourth distinction that can be used on our problem. The distinction is between the end of the work or action (*finis operis*) and the end of the worker or agent (*finis operantis*). Here is an example. A sculptor makes a statue of Lincoln in order to make money (*finis operantis*). But this desire for money in no way touches the necessity he is under to make a statue that looks like Lincoln (*finis operis*). This second factor—the statue's likeness to Lincoln—is determined by the Lincoln that once lived. The end of the work is a statue like Lincoln. The end of the worker is money to be earned. The possible ways in which the end of the work is related to the end of the intelligent worker are many. (1) They can coincide, as when the sculptor desires merely the expression of his idea of Lincoln; (2) they can be distinct, as when he wishes to make money; (3) the end of the work can be the same while the end of agent can be many—for example, two sculptors make a statue of Lincoln, but one intends to make money thereby, the other to please his friends; (4) the one end of the worker can be the same for different works, each with its own end—for example, in order to make money, the worker makes a statue of Lincoln, raises chickens, and writes plays. Notice the upshot of this multiple relation of the two types of ends of human action. There is no necessary connection between any end of a work and the end of the worker because freedom bears on this precise point. Man freely sets his own ends, short, of course, of his ultimate end; and even here he decides in what he will find his ultimate end.

The distinction between the end of the work and the end of the worker would be used by one who sets out to explain a Catholic college by going back to the founder of the college. Thus if the founder of the college intended to make his students better Christians, then moral virtue is the end of the founder, and knowledge is the end of the college. As a description of the facts, this statement seems to be perfectly sound. As an explanation, it leaves untouched the very issue to be resolved; that is, how does a liberal arts college foster or train to virtue? Not merely because the end of the founder was to develop better Christians. With the same end in view he could have chosen to administer the sacraments or found sodalities for workmen or give retreats to businessmen or do most anything short of sin. There is no necessary line going from any end of the worker to the end of his work, other than the general one that they be not mutually exclusive (for example, to wish to please God by blaspheming). All other connections go the other way: the end of the work can determine under what ends of the worker it will intelligently function. If a religious founder chose a liberal arts college as the work he thought would issue in moral virtue, the reason must be that such a college, properly set up, can issue in virtue. Then the founder was faced with the same question that we are: What in a college fosters moral virtue? His intention does not solve this issue. What his intention does account for is the existence of the college, whatever be its peculiar organization or activities. There would be no "this college" unless he intended it to foster moral virtue. But his intention that the college aid moral virtue does not achieve the virtue; what it achieves is the college. Consequently, we, like the founder, are still faced with our original question: How does a liberal arts college relate itself to moral virtue?

The last of the clarifying distinctions we propose to consider is that of primary and secondary end. We mentioned above, when considering direct and indirect objectives, that the primary-secondary and direct-indirect distinctions deal with the same matter; that is, action and end. Direct-indirect emphasizes the data from the viewpoint of action's relation to end, since the action is direct or indirect. Primary-secondary emphasizes the end's relation to action, since the end determines the action, and it is this determination that is named primary or secondary. Thus ends, not actions, are primary and secondary.

The end, of course, does not determine action except through the agent. Agents are attracted by the end, drawn into an action which is such that it can achieve the end by which they are attracted. In this sense the end determines the action. Notice that two points come in here. The first is that of the relation of end to agent. This relation takes on special significance where agents are free to decide their own ends. Men freely decide what their ends will be. To distinguish here between primary and secondary end will be of little help, since the final reason why any end is primary in this sense is that the man so decided it would be. The second point is that of the relation of the end to the action. Some actions will achieve certain ends and some will not. The action of writing, for instance, will produce written words; the action of talking will not. Freedom has nothing to do with this relation of action to its product except to respect it. Now look at this same relation from the viewpoint of the end. That is, the end, words written, gives possibility and form to the action of writing, and does so even before the action of writing takes place. If, for instance, written words were impossible, there could be no action of writing at all. The possibility of written words founds the possibility of the action of writing. Again, if written words could be only one syllable, all writing actions would have to be one-syllable writing; and if, in addition, writing could be only in ink, all writing would be one-syllable writing in ink. This is what we mean by saying that the end gives form to action and makes it possible. And the end that makes an action possible and most fully determines its form or kind would be the primary end. Any other end that may happen to modify the form of the action would be called a secondary end.

What we have been saying is that primary and secondary are a distinction applied to the end with reference to the action and are not a distinction that applies to the end with reference to the free agent. The same point can be stated in the framework of the distinction, made above, of the end of the worker (*finis operantis*) and the end of the work (*finis operis*). Primary and secondary have no power of explanation when applied to the end of the worker, the end of the free agent. What explanatory value they have comes from being applied to the end of the work or action. This means that any discussion of primary and secondary ends must be divorced from the intention of the free agent. To shift back and forth between the end of the agent and the end of the action will knot up any consideration of primary and secondary ends. Yet it is easy to do this, temptingly easy. We shall be at pains not to fall into this fallacy; our consideration of primary and secondary ends will be held to the end of the work or action.

There are some meanings of primary and secondary that merely have to be mentioned in order to be excluded from our present discussion. One such is the use of *primary end* to mean *ultimate end*,[8] all other ends being secondary. In this sense neither human knowledge nor virtue is a primary end of education, for each, like education itself, is only a means to the primary (ultimate) end. This primary end of all human actions is the same: perfect happiness, or possession of infinite being and good, or the beatific vision. Clearly, this end, as what crowns ultimately every human action, does not serve the relatively minor purpose of specifying this or that kind of action. Its work is more exalted, to justify there being action at all. To ask the ultimate end to specify and distinguish the actions of teaching from other actions is to ask not so much the impossible as the unworthy. Lesser ends justify their title to being ends at all precisely by doing the lesser work of specifying what this or that action will be. Since our consideration hits precisely on the kind of actions that make up schooling, appeal to the ultimate end will not be of direct help to us at present.

Another usage that can be excluded quickly is that in which *primary* means "important" and *secondary* means "unimportant." No one, least of all a Catholic, would seriously maintain that virtue is unimportant for college students, just as no one would publicly propose to give college degrees to good boys and girls whether they know anything or not. No doubt this may happen in practice. In fact, this practical position is the special temptation of any church-related school, owing assuredly to the fact that the love of God and man is the reason why such colleges were started at all. The very reluctance, however, to take such a position openly is indication that it is not considered particularly reasonable by those who may happen to adopt it. Consequently there seems to be no demand that we discuss it here.

We shall go now to the classic use of primary and secondary end. It is found in considerations of Christian marriage. Descriptively, marriage is the full union of a man and woman that sets up a common life naturally helpful to both parents and naturally issuing, unless nature is defective, in offspring requiring care and training. Catholic moral theologians call the birth and care of offspring the primary or principal end of marriage; and they call the mutually helpful common life the secondary end of marriage.[9] Marriage, in such discussions, is considered a state of life composed of many actions. Thus the word "end" used of a state of life may have to be modified from its precise meaning when applied to one action. In a discussion of the end of marriage one can, however, shift the question to one distinctive action and speak of sexual union, even though moral theologians generally do not speak of one action but of marriage.

The two ends of marriage—the procreation and raising of children, and a mutually helpful common life—are both ends of the action (*finis operis*) and may or may not in fact be ends of the agents (*fines operantium*). Both are essential; neither is accidental or unimportant. The secondary end (mutually helpful common life) is essentially dependent on the primary end and is an end at all only because it is subordinate to the primary. The secondary end serves the purpose of attaining the primary end more certainly and surely. The two must always be kept together as necessarily connected, the secondary necessarily subordinate to the primary.[10]

There are other ways of stating this position on marriage. If one looks at marriage as a state, he would say that the primary and secondary ends are not so much two fully distinct ends as one end in its imperfect and perfect stage. The perfect stage of the end, children born and raised, is more completely the end because it more specifies the state and its actions. For marriage is not just any kind of common life of persons but one that is by nature ordered to the procreation and raising of children. Yet this perfect stage of the end can be attained only by another good in itself; that is, the good of a mutually helpful common life. Thus the end of marriage has a preliminary or imperfect end as well as a complete and perfect end. Again, if one looks at the marriage act, sexual union, one could say that the secondary and primary are two aspects of one end. The mutually helpful common life is one aspect of this action's end and the procreation (and later raising) of offspring another aspect of the same end. This statement holds in a unity all the facts that moral theologians account for by distinguishing between the primary and secondary end. So also does the statement that speaks of imperfect and perfect stage of one end.

Now this meaning of primary and secondary, developed to explain marriage, does little for the question of knowledge and virtue in college teaching no matter how the distinction is stated. Knowledge is not the imperfect stage of virtue, nor is virtue the imperfect stage of knowledge. Nor are knowledge and virtue two aspects of the same thing. Finally, neither virtue nor knowledge is subordinated to the other so that one is a good only when subordinated to the other and dependent on it. In other words, the classic meaning of primary and secondary is not applicable to our problem.

There is, however, one meaning of the distinction that is applicable. Take the primary end to be one that an action properly attains and that no other action properly attains; take the secondary end to be one that an action may or may not attain and that other actions may properly attain. Using this meaning, one can say that teaching properly attains knowledge as its primary end. This statement says exactly what was said above about the direct objective. For primary end is what is attained directly, and the secondary is what is attained indirectly. And, having rejected the direct-indirect distinction, we shall have to reject this meaning of primary and secondary for the very same reasons. These reasons, recall, were two. First, the indirect objective (secondary end) becomes relatively unimportant and nonessential—nonessential because it may not be attained by the action. On this showing, virtue would become nonessential to teaching. Second, the indirect objective (secondary end), when attained, would be attained by the same action that attained the primary end. On this showing, knowledge would be the cause, although indirect, of virtue. Recall also that both of these positions are invitations to add to the college program some activities that will cause virtue directly. If this state of affairs is unsatisfactory, the distinction of primary and secondary end is no help in solving our problem.

Notice that each of the clarifying distinctions considered so far—direct-indirect, proximate-remote, end of works and of workers, primary-secondary—sets up a dichotomy. Each distinction supplies two classes or categories. With two candidates, knowledge and virtue, for classification and two opposed categories for the candidates, it seems merely a problem of finding the right slot for each candidate. Thus one can find reasons for saying that the college's primary, direct, and proximate end is knowledge. Another finds reasons for saying that virtue (and the life of grace) is the primary, direct, and proximate end of the college. Let the two men argue. When all is finished the winner will still have won only a battle, not the war.

There are more battles in store for either victor. Let knowledge be the primary, direct, and proximate end of the college. No matter how much sense this makes, its correlative, that virtue is the secondary, indirect, and remote end, makes too little sense. And one who has to defend this last statement has a long campaign before him. Or let virtue be the primary, direct, and proximate end of the college. No matter how much sense this makes, its correlative, that knowledge is the secondary, indirect, and remote end, makes too little sense. Another long campaign is the only prospect. For it seems that neither knowledge nor virtue can be a secondary, indirect, and remote end of a Catholic college. Then one wonders what the advantage is of affirming that either virtue or knowledge is the primary, direct, and proximate end of a college.

At this point, the reader may be annoyed to find his favorite distinction dispossessed. But this should not be too disconcerting. Distinctions serve to classify. In some situations the things or actions we are considering fall into our classes neatly. Our effort at distinguishing pays off in such cases. There is no guarantee, however, that such distinctions, or any distinction for that matter, will handle all facts. When they fail us, love of our formerly helpful distinctions should not blind us to the prior right of the facts. If the facts escape our distinction, the only wise path open is to discard the familiar distinction for a better one, if such can be found. Primary-secondary, direct-indirect, proximate-remote, end of work-worker, seem to be candidates for discard when one is talking of knowledge and virtue in a liberal arts college.

The reason why these distinctions fail to apply fully is the "nature" of the college. That is, it really is not a nature. Natural things, substances given in nature, have a definite constitution with powers ordered to definite activities towards a set end. A turtle egg, for example, has a set structure or nature ordered to developing into a grown turtle. Its activity of growing has an intrinsic finality, an order of action (growing) to an end (turtle) that, barring outside interference, is guaranteed by its very constitution. When considering natural substances and their activities, it makes perfect sense to talk of primary, direct, proximate ends. A college, though, is not a natural substance. It has no set nature or essence proper to itself and consequently no end in the precise sense that a turtle egg has. The college is a social creation arising from human desires and decisions.[11] The structure and function it has are partly determined by human decisions. And human decisions themselves are influenced and modified by social and cultural conditions in which the men, and their colleges, exist. Consequently there is no essence or absolute nature called a college. Consequently, too, there is no absolute primary, direct, and proximate end of a college.

Having noted this fact, we must state immediately that though men make colleges, they can only make successfully when they respect the natures of the things and activities they employ. No carpenter in his right mind would expect his miter box to saw wood, any more than an artist would expect his painting strokes to shape marble. *A pari*, no founder of a college can reasonably expect acts of fraternal charity to result in knowledge of physics, any more than he can expect the study of physics to result in the virtue of charity. Activities have their natural and intrinsic finality. Teaching that does not deal with knowledge is not teaching. Wishing will never change that. Acts of moral virtue that do not deal with the good to be done are not acts of virtue. Nor will wishing change this. Every activity has its proper end, and this end must be respected. The price paid for not respecting the proper end of an activity is the futility of failure.

But this is not the only kind of failure. A second kind consists in forgetting that activities can be brought into an existential union with other and different activities in order to achieve the purposes of men. And this union, while respecting the natures of the unified activities, modifies and molds the activities united. After this the joined activities can no longer be fully described without including their role in the union. Thus a college unifies the activities judged important in developing the powers of the young. Whatever these may be—and we are interested in only those ordered to knowledge and virtue—they will be modified by being a part of a college. Teaching and knowledge will now be saturated with moral factors; moral actions will now be saturated with knowledge factors. For teaching isolated from all moral considerations would not be fully perfective of the young; just as moral choices isolated from all growth in knowledge would not be fully perfective of the young who are gaining more knowledge. Both factors must be present in every activity the college performs. And present not only in fact but also in our understanding and explanation of the fact.

That is why the four distinctions considered above were judged inadequate. Each in its own way tried to separate (in understanding) knowledge and virtue as if they were two peas in one pod. But if you separate knowledge and virtue as two things (or ends), then neither can be the objective of a college. The framework of college education —that is, activities perfective of the young—demands that the knowledge taught and learned there be the knowledge of a virtuous man, just as it demands that the virtue exercised be that of a knowing man. Neither knowledge nor virtue as an object of college education is related to the other as its equal and opposite.

CHAPTER 3

KNOWLEDGE

AND ITS STATE

BY POSSESSION

The last chapter concluded that neither knowledge nor virtue has an undisputed right to be the primary, direct, and proximate end of a college. We suggested instead that a college was equally interested in knowledge and in virtue—in knowledge as that which it could teach and in virtue as the condition of the possession of such knowledge. That is, the clarifying distinction being proposed is between knowledge and the state of its possession.[1] We must now try to validate this distinction, first in its own right and then with reference to the college.

Any distinction applicable to knowledge will have to be grounded in the nature of knowledge. Thus some description or definition of knowledge is needed at this point.[2] Suppose we begin with examples. Consider these statements: "The old man died of pneumonia"; "Ball-point pens quickly run out of ink"; "To open, press down on the center of the top." All of these cases of knowledge have it in common that they give an account of something. The first accounts for the man's death; the second, for one weakness of ball-point pens; the third, for the way to open the jar. Moreover, the three accounts achieve the purpose of the act of knowing. If knowing is directed to the cause of the old man's death, the purpose of the knowing act is achieved by the account given; that is, pneumonia is the cause. If the purpose of knowing is directed to how to open the jar, the account given—press down on the center of the top— achieves that purpose. Such an account is a proper account, since it achieves the purpose of knowing. And knowledge can be defined as a proper account of something, an account that achieves the purpose of knowing.

Notice we say that a proper account is one that achieves the purpose of knowing, not the purpose of the knower. The purpose or purposes of the knower may or may not be achieved by a proper account. In the example given above, the knower may wish to know the cause of the old man's death in order to collect insurance. The knower's purpose is to collect insurance, and this is not achieved by the knowledge of the cause of his death. What is achieved is the purpose of the knowing, since this was directed to the cause of death and this was attained. Of course, the two purposes, of knower and of knowing, may coincide. Say, the knower wishes to know how to open the jelly jar. Then the account—namely, to press down on the center of the top—will attain both purposes. But it is a proper account because it achieves the purpose of knowing.

The purpose of knowing will be either to know what is true about something or how to do or make something. The first, what is true about something, is called theoretical or speculative knowledge. Both adjectives have the same root meaning. *Theoretical* is from a Greek verb meaning "to look at"; *speculative* is from a Latin verb meaning the same thing. Since this knowledge deals with what is, the knower looks at the facts and says what he sees. Thus, the old man died of pneumonia; and knowledge stating what is true about the old man's death is speculative knowledge. The second kind of account, how to do or make, is called practical knowledge, from a Greek verb meaning "to do or manage." This knowledge deals with what is to be done, not with what is. The act of knowing is not one of looking at what is but of knowing how to get something into existence. Granted that you want to take the top off the jar, you need to know how to get it off. The knowledge of how to get it off—that is, by pressing down on the center of the top—is practical knowledge.

It is always necessary to make this distinction between speculative and practical knowledge. The two kinds of knowledge have their important differences. The knowledge by which we say what is, is controlled ultimately by what is. The beginning point of such knowledge is the existent. Given a thing, we can possibly say what it is; without it there would be nothing to say. If we miss what it is, our knowledge is not true. These facts are neatly summarized by saying that the existent (being) is the first principle or controlling factor of theoretical knowledge. In less precise terms, we say that knowledge should be objective, that one should stick to the facts. (We refer, of course, to speculative knowledge.) Practical knowledge, by contrast, is quite different from theoretical. First of all, this knowledge can hardly begin with what exists since its whole purpose is to bring something into existence. The mechanic building a car begins with metal and tools, and intends to convert the metal into a car that does not yet exist; the painter, using paint and canvas, intends to convert these into a painting that does not yet exist. Thus the necessary supposition of practical knowledge is that the object does not exist.

The second important difference between practical and speculative knowledge is that in practical knowledge the knower wants the object to exist. This introduces a brand-new factor into knowledge: desire. The mechanic desires the car to exist; the artist desires his painting to exist. And since desire deals with good (able to be desired), practical or making knowledge deals with the good. Moreover, the good is the starting point of this knowledge. If nothing seemed good, there would be no knowledge about making. We set out to make something because we think it is worthwhile; that is, it is good for it to be. Of course, there is no makable thing that is just good in general or goodness. The goods open to our desires (and our making) are good existents. Cars have to be cars as the necessary and

obvious condition of their being good as cars are. This is
the way things or existents came into practical knowledge.
They came in under the guise of a good thing or the desirable thing. Thus practical knowledge has two principles or
controlling factors, the good of the object and the object
which is good. In less precise language we say that if one
wants something hard enough, one will get it done. Here
we stress the "good" factor. We also say that wishing is not
enough unless one has know-how. Here we stress the
"thing" factor, since know-how arises from considering the
characteristics that a thing must have in order to be that
particular thing.

Notice that speculative and practical knowledge have
quite different norms of rectitude. What controls speculative knowledge is the object or thing known. Speculative
knowledge, to be good knowledge, must say what the
thing is. Thus the thing is the norm or measure, and the
knowledge must suit itself to the thing; it is, in other
words, measured by the object. Practical knowledge, by
contrast, is itself the norm or measure, and the thing made
must suit the knowledge; the thing made, that is, is measured by the knowledge.

The artist's knowledge, since it is the cause of the effect,
controls and determines or measures what the effect, the
thing made, will be. Practical knowledge is causative
knowledge; speculative knowledge is not and cannot be
causative. There is always the temptation to think of speculative knowledge as a first stage and practical knowledge
as a second stage of the same kind of knowledge. That is,
you begin with speculative knowledge, add the will or desiring factor, and the union constitutes practical knowledge. This view supposes that the artist, for instance, first

has a thought (speculative knowledge) and then the desire to make that thought exist on his canvas (practical knowledge). On this showing, practical knowledge is not knowledge at all but only willing added to speculation; nor is speculative knowledge strictly speculative, since it, too, would treat of what can be done or made. What is, is not makable, since it already is. And knowledge of what is, is not and cannot be practical, no matter what is added to it. Its object already exists and is therefore not makable at all. The object of practical knowledge does not exist but can be made to exist. The wide difference between what is and cannot be made and what is not but can be made is the basis for the wide difference between speculative and practical knowledge.

Anyone, therefore, who finds it necessary to look closer at knowledge will have to take two steps: one, look at speculative; two, look at practical knowledge. This necessity will control our consideration. We have raised the question about the difference between knowledge and its state of possession. If there is such a difference, it will have to be located in each knowledge separately. Our present task is therefore cut out for us. We shall begin our consideration with practical knowledge.

For purposes of analysis take the practical knowledge of surgery. As knowledge, it is the art of correcting deformities and injuries by manual and instrumental operations. Now, suppose this knowledge of surgery is possessed by two doctors. Both are first-rate surgeons, possessing excellent knowledge of surgery. They differ, however, in this, that one is a virtuous doctor, who uses his knowledge of surgery to save human lives; the other is vicious and uses his knowledge of surgery to produce criminal abortions.

These men differ as healer from killer. But their knowledge of surgery, as knowledge, does not differ. Both know how to heal by means of instrumental operations; both, by supposition, know surgery equally well. The difference, therefore, between the two is not in their knowledge of surgery. Yet a difference there is, a huge difference. In the healer, the knowledge of surgery is possessed by a virtuous man, and his use of the knowledge perfects him as a man. In the killer, the knowledge of surgery is possessed by a vicious man, and his use of the knowledge makes him more vicious. In one sense, the knowledge of surgery in both is the same, insofar as it is knowledge. In another sense, the knowledge of surgery differs in the two men as the perfective differs from the destructive. Yet the difference arises from the state of its possession; it does not arise from the knowledge itself.

A closer look at the killer will reveal the factors that specify the way he possesses his knowledge of surgery. Considered in itself, surgery, because it is practical knowledge, is knowledge of actions to an end. The end is to correct deformities so that the body can heal itself. The actions are such as will attain this end. This is true of surgery as a body of knowledge; that is, in the abstract. But in fact there is nothing in the knowledge of such actions that guarantees they will be ordered to health or even that they will be actions at all. A man could know surgery and never use it. Since nothing in the knowledge forces him to use it, there is nothing in surgery forcing him to use it for the end of health. He can simply ignore health as an end, and this leaves him open to try for some other end. But in order to do this he must positively and willfully ignore the reasonable ordering of surgery, for this ordering is obvious. Together with his knowledge of actions of surgery he must willfully ignore the end of such actions. Thus the state of possession of his knowledge of surgery is resultant upon an act of the will, bad will. He freely chooses to ignore the obvious end of surgical actions.

The virtuous doctor, however, possesses the knowledge of surgery with no willed ignoring of the end of the actions of surgery. His will does not step in to separate actions from their proper end; he wills to have surgical actions attain health. Just as with the killer, nothing in his knowledge of surgery forces him to order surgical actions to health. Yet he does, and he does so by an act of the will. Thus the state of this doctor's possession of the knowledge of surgery is one brought about by an act of the will, good will.

In the example we have used, the factor that determined the state of the possession of practical knowledge is a free choice. The surgical knowledge of the killer and the healer differ by an act of will, which changes not the knowledge but the state of its possession. Moreover, this state of possession itself determines the perfectible or destructible character of such knowledge. With bad will the knowledge of surgery can lead to the destruction of the human character of its possessor. With good will the knowledge of surgery can lead to the perfection of the human character of its possessor.

Notice that we are here talking about human character, not the human mind. All knowledge, because it is knowledge, perfects the human mind, which is a power of knowing. But knowledge, merely because it is knowledge, does not necessarily perfect the man. It did not in the case of the killer. His knowledge of surgery made him a worse man in himself and more dangerous to society than he would have been without such knowledge. Notice, too, that what we have said of the practical knowledge of surgery is applicable only to practical knowledge—and only to such practical knowledge as does not guarantee its own good use.[3] Our first conclusion, then, is that the state of the possession of such practical knowledge is not determined by the knowledge but by an act of the will. Our second conclusion is that the state of possession determines the power of such knowledge to perfect the man possessing it.

When we turn to speculative knowledge, a different situation presents itself. There is no question here of willing to ignore the end of the knowledge. Speculative knowledge does not attain an end beyond itself. It is neutral with regard to ends because it is not concerned with doing or making. Since speculative knowledge is about what is, not about the achievable, it can achieve nothing because it does not make its object exist, as practical knowledge does. Among the kinds of speculative knowledge, the one least related to an end is mathematics. Mathematics is about what is; and what it is about is conceived so abstractly and universally that its objects could never be made to exist outside the mind. No one, for instance, could make a strict mathematical triangle, though he can make chalk ones on the board or iron ones for dinner gongs. A strict mathematical triangle would have to be constituted by lines of no thickness, and such lines cannot be constituted except in the mind, where they are not lines but thought-of lines. This fully abstract character of mathematics makes it a test case for our consideration of speculative knowledge.

For this consideration let us imagine two men, one of whom is an expert mathematician but also an unjust man, a thief; the other man is equally expert in mathematics and is a just man besides. There is no question of the thief's using his mathematics, say, to determine the charge necessary to blast open the door of a safe. If this were the fact to be considered, our case turns out nearly the same as that taken above in practical knowledge. There is no point in considering that again. In our present example we are considering speculative knowledge in its purity. We look only to the knowledge of mathematics in the just and the unjust man, not to how either uses this knowledge in order to attain some end. Thus our fact is only that a just and an unjust man both have expert mathematical knowledge.

Is there any way to distinguish the mathematical knowledge of these two men? By supposition, both are equally good mathematicians. There is no factor here of willed ignoring of ends; the only factor is knowledge. Between the one knowledge and the other, as knowledge, there seems to be no difference at all.[4] Both are equal; both deal with the same objects; both are equally perfective of the minds of the two men. This point was raised above. Knowledge perfects the mind of its possessor; where knowledge is equal, it equally perfects the mind. But is it true that knowledge perfects the whole man? We said above that it does not. And here we must consider this more closely, since the only difference between the one knowledge and the other is the difference between the mathematical knowledge of a good man and that of a bad man.

Our immediate question can be stated: Why does not purely speculative knowledge perfect the whole man? I have stated the question in this sharp way in order to exclude the answer that, other things being equal, speculative knowledge perfects man. That is, if two men are good men and one knows mathematics while the other does not, the knower of mathematics is the better man. The trouble with this answer is that it answers a question no one need ever ask. All agree that knowledge perfects the mind; and that is all the above answer can rightfully mean. The problem, however, is why speculative knowledge does not perfect the whole man.

A number of preliminary steps are needed to see and answer the question. First, the perfection of man. Man is not born perfect in any sense, which means that his perfection is something over and above what he begins existence with. Were he born perfect, we would say that his perfection is so identified with himself that if he is, he is perfect. Such is the case with mathematical figures and numbers. They are perfect from the beginning; they neither grow nor wear out; they cannot be improved because they are from the start all they can ever be. Also, they have no powers of acting. If they did, there would be nothing for the powers to do. Man, however, is a being with powers of acting. He can grow; he can know; he can choose. If his powers are not used, to that extent he is not what he can be; that is, he is less than what is open to him and therefore perfectible by what he can be.

Perfectibility is thus in man. But what perfects him cannot be in him. If it were, he would already be perfect, not perfectible. The very state of perfectibility, as a potential state, demands that what perfects man be other than he. He must therefore seek and acquire something other than himself—he cannot acquire himself—in order to improve or perfect himself. Take growth as an example. A man's body can grow. But it grows on what is outside itself. Thus it seeks and acquires food, which it then uses so that possible growth becomes actual growth. Food stands with reference to possible growth as the outsider that can issue in the perfection of full growth. When food is possessed, man actually grows. Such an outsider is called a good; we say that food is good. This outsider answers the inclination or desire to growth; we call what answers an inclination or desire an end. Thus food is an end, an outside good that is sought and possessed in order to complete or perfect the being acting.

The above example, unsatisfactory from many viewpoints—growth is not one of the top activities of man—is nevertheless pointed in regard to what an end is for man. First, it is something other than man, something added to him. That a man's good should be other than he arises from his perfectibility and consequent need of an addition to be what he can be. Second, an end is sought because it can be identified with man. Where food is concerned, the identification is physical. Food becomes a part of the physical nature of man. Not all goods can become physically a part of man. But the goods, in order to be an end for a man, must be identified with the man. How else would such additions perfect him? Food not possessed will not result in growth. The virtue of justice not possessed will not make a man just. The only way a good can possibly perfect man is by having it in some way be him or him be it. Where the good is material, the identification of man and the added good must be a material identification. Where the good is immaterial, the identification will have to be immaterial.

Immaterial identification is an act of choice. By choice I make a good be my good by so deciding that it will be. An example will help here. Consider a man faced with two different goods, to get married or stay single. Each has its attractive aspects, so that getting married seems good for one set of reasons and staying single seems good for another set of reasons. As yet the man has not chosen either the good of marriage or the good of a single life. Then he chooses, say, to get married. This choice consists in making one of these goods the good for him. That is, he identifies the good of marriage with himself. To remain single, still a good, is not now his good. Nor need he deny, in order to make the choice, that the single life is good. He may well agree that it is very good. But right now a single life is not for him. It is not what he wants to identify himself with at this moment. He has, of course, reasons for choosing to marry. But his reasons for marrying do not fully account for his choice, since there were reasons, and good ones, for not marrying—namely, the reasons for staying single. Thus reasons alone cannot account for his actual choice, for reasons could also have accounted for the opposite choice of not getting married. The way to express this situation is to say that he had reasons for his choice to marry but that these reasons do not account for their being his reasons for marrying. What makes these reasons his is his accepting them as his own. In other words, accepting the reasons for marrying is the way he identifies himself with the good of marriage. If reasons controlled choice fully, there would be no self-identification; at most there would be rational consistency, and choices would be ignorant or well-informed, not good or bad. And self would have nothing to do in choice except to keep reasons on file and ready for reference, like a mechanical brain.

Choice is a self-commitment to a good other than self. When I choose, I take sides. I put myself on the side of the good I desire in order to possess whatever it has. There is no other way to possess its goodness except by bringing it to myself. First, I bring it to myself internally, and therefore immaterially, by my desiring it. The good I want exists in my desire of it. This is the point at which I first identify myself with a good. Beyond that, I try to bring it to myself in a physical and material way whenever this is possible. The goods to which I do not commit myself remain disconnected from me. They affect me in no way; they do not perfect me at all.

Now we have what is necessary in order to consider the problem raised above; namely, why speculative knowledge does not perfect the whole man. Recall what we have said. First, what perfects the whole man will have to be something other than he. Second, this something must be united to man so that it is identified with himself or, what comes to the same, he identifies himself with it. We shall test speculative knowledge against each of these requirements.

Speculative knowledge deals with what is other than the knower. All knowledge implies a knower and a known, a subject knowing and an object known. For the subject to know itself, it must in some way make itself into an object. Thus there is always an equivalent "other" in speculative knowledge. To the extent that knowledge introduces something into man, to that extent it can be perfective of man.

But the second requirement, that of identifying self with this other, seems to find no place in speculative knowledge. As we said above, speculative knowledge says what is, and being therefore is the first principle and norm of such knowledge. Being is neither mine nor yours; it is open to all. It stands as that to which the mind must be conformed, if speculative knowledge is to be true. Thus identification of self with such an object becomes pointless. I may prefer as mine (in other words, identify with myself) that two and two should be five, but nothing happens if I do. Two and two remain four, whether I like it or not. The reason is that speculative knowledge is a union of the subject with the other (object) as other (object and not self). Self-identification, by contrast, is a union of the subject with the other (object) as self. Now, an object identified with self is what an end is. For ends are goods that selves have chosen as theirs. Speculative knowledge will never make an object exist. Only choice will do this, as we said earlier.

No one should take the last paragraph as saying that speculative knowledge is not itself good and therefore a possible end. It is good to know mathematics, and one can choose to know it. In fact, he will never know it unless he does so choose. But his choice to know mathematics is not itself the knowledge of mathematics. His choice is one thing and his knowledge of mathematics is another. The latter is speculative knowledge and is achieved by con-formity of the mind to mathematical objects; the former is choice and is achieved by self-identification. Again, no one should think that speculative knowledge cannot be knowledge of what is good. It certainly can because it does. But knowing what the good is, is not making this good be identified with self. Human experience is too full of such failures to need further emphasis here.

We can now give, by way of summary, an answer to the question why speculative knowledge is not fully perfective of man. Man must be perfected by attaining an end out-side himself. Speculative knowledge may help him know this end, but it cannot be the action by which he attains it. In order to attain the end he must identify a good with himself. This is done only by an act of choice or commitment. Thus man will fully perfect himself by choices, not unrelated to speculative knowledge but nevertheless beyond speculative knowledge.[5]

Let us return to the example that raised the question of speculative knowledge and the perfectibility of the whole man. We were considering two mathematicians, one just and the other unjust. We supposed that there was no difference in the quality and extent of their knowledge of mathematics. There is a difference, however, in the state of the possession of the knowledge. One knowledge exists in the mind of a man who is just; the other in one who is unjust. These states, of being just or unjust, are not produced by mathematics but by free choice, made with no dependence on mathematical knowledge. Nor do these states of justice or injustice either improve or impair the mathematical excellence of the knowledge in either man. They do, however, improve or impair the men possessing such knowledge. By determining the state of the possession of mathematical knowledge these states become vitally important in college teaching.

The reason is clear enough. The only justification for any school is that it should improve or perfect students. The perfection of the student includes not only speculative knowledge; it also includes the state of this knowledge. Recall that speculative knowledge is not fully perfective of man. Man is perfected by choices that modify the knowledge by determining the state of the possession of such knowledge. A school, by reason of its special finality, is ordered to knowledge perfective of students. Such knowledge, to be fully perfective, must be possessed in a state that is itself perfective. If the state of possession is not perfective, what serious justification can be found for teaching and schools? To answer this question, imagine a student body composed entirely of the vicious. What would justify teaching them, unless there were the possibility that such teaching might reduce their viciousness, if only by keeping them occupied with something worthwhile? To make the vicious more capably vicious is not a worthy action. Even from the viewpoint of enlightened self-interest such action does not make sense. And this is one way of admitting that the state of possession of knowledge is just as important to the act of teaching as the knowledge taught. If one wishes to discuss knowledge in the abstract, he can say that knowledge is perfective of the human mind no matter what its state of possession might be. Such discussion has its place, and we shall come to it later. But when knowledge is to be discussed in the framework of education and schooling, to ignore the state of its possession is to leave out part of the relation of knowledge to the perfectibility of the student. And this relation is precisely at the center of teaching.

I have been at pains to validate the distinction between knowledge, either practical or speculative, and the state of its possession. I have not tried to give all the factors that determine the state of possession of knowledge. In both practical and speculative knowledge I limited consideration to acts of choice as determining the state of possession of knowledge. There are others, not acts of choice; some of these we shall have occasion to consider. At present, the need is to see that there is such a distinction and that it must be applied when considering the school, since schools are ordered to teaching and learning that shall be as perfective of the young as possible.

The distinctions that we rejected in the last chapter, as not applying to our question of knowledge and virtue in college teaching, all had the defect of setting up a dichotomy—primary-secondary, direct-indirect, proper-not proper, proximate-remote, and of work and the worker. The distinction between knowledge and its state of possession is not a dichotomy. Dichotomies are constituted by opposition between two units. In logic, whence the term derives its meaning, the first condition of a dichotomy is that the two opposed be perfections of the same sort. Black and white constitute a dichotomy; black cannot be white, nor can a black thing be a white thing. Both black and white are qualities of the same sort, kinds of color. Also, the dichotomy, white and black, is between two of the same sort, since black is a denial in the area of color. But there can be no dichotomy between two perfections in different areas. Between tall and friendly, or between learned and skinny, or between clever and wealthy there is no dichotomy possible. None is possible because any one man could be any two of them simultaneously. A dichotomy, to be of any use to understanding, must precisely separate two things or two characteristics of things in such a way that one excludes the other. Where there is no exclusion of one by the other, there may be difference but not a difference that constitutes a dichotomy.

The distinctions rejected in the last chapter were rejected because they were proposed as dichotomies. Direct-indirect, proper-not proper, immediate (proximate)-mediate (remote), primary-secondary, were all examples of dichotomies. No end can be both of these simultaneously; if an end is one of these opposites, it cannot be the other. The distinction between the end of the work and end of the worker need not be a dichotomy, since the two can coincide, as we said in Chapter 2. But when the two are different and proposed because different—knowledge as end of teaching and virtue as end of teacher—the result is a dichotomy. Both are ends and one is not the other. The distinction defended here, between knowledge and the state of its possession, is not a dichotomy. The first condition, that both perfections should be of the same sort, is not fulfilled. Moreover, there is no opposition; if there were, knowledge could never exist in a human mind. For any one truth that comes to a human mind must come into a person characterized both by other knowledge he may happen to have and by qualities that are not knowledge. These qualities constitute the framework in which new knowledge must reside in this person. Not only is this framework not exclusive of knowledge; it is the very condition of acquiring knowledge not already possessed. There is a difference between knowledge and the state of its possession; there can be no dichotomy between them.

Nor need there be a dichotomy of means, one set of means, that is, for producing knowledge and a contrary set to encourage virtue (status of possession of knowledge). There can be such. Any society can encourage its members to make good choices, and no society can be totally uninterested in the virtue of its members. Colleges are not exceptions. They, too, can and generally do introduce some activities of this sort. But the situation is not that colleges must add extracurricular nonteaching activities as the major means to take care of the state of possession of the knowledge. This is not the situation because the act of teaching concerns itself both with the knowledge taught and the state of its possession. And this causality of teaching, operative day in and day out, is so tied in with the knowledge gained that at times the two are indistinguishable. Extracurricular activities hold the place of a Johnny-come-lately. They are introduced after the knowledge and its state of possession are pretty well set. They can reinforce and clarify, by directed personal experience, what has been done in the classroom; they cannot undo it or supply for it.

The last paragraph contains statements so far not supported by reasons. These reasons will take up the rest of this volume. The proposition to be established is that the Catholic college in its very act of teaching concerns itself with both knowledge and the state of its possession. Read "state of possession" as meaning especially those factors (surrounding acquired knowledge) that pertain to moral virtue, and understand "moral virtue" to mean doing the will of God. The proposition, then, is this: The Catholic college precisely as a college and in its acts of teaching concerns itself with the knowledge and with the virtue of its students.

The statement of the position leaves something to be desired. It still encourages one to reintroduce the distinctions excluded in Chapter 2. Those distinctions—primary-secondary, direct-indirect, and so on—arose when one considered the data from the agent through the action to the end. Our statement of the proposition has the same form; it proceeds from the college (agent) through teaching (action) to the student's knowledge and virtue (end). In such a statement the data will always present a temptation to reintroduce the excluded distinctions. What is worse, the statement invites one to misunderstand the act of teaching itself.

It is a misunderstanding of teaching to think of it as something in the teacher. For example, it is easy to think that a good teacher is one who possesses certain qualities of mind and character, and a bad teacher as one who lacks these. But the good qualities of the teacher do not guarantee teaching, either good or bad. Imagine the case of the excellent teacher lecturing brilliantly to an empty classroom. Whatever the man is doing, he is not teaching. The reason is that no one is learning. Now, learning is the only guarantee of good teaching because it constitutes good teaching. What we are saying is that teaching is a transient activity and, like all such actions, must reside in its perfect stage in the recipient. That is, teaching in its complete and perfect state resides in the student taught. If the student has learned from the teacher, the teaching is fully good. If the student has not learned, the teaching is incomplete, no matter where the blame may lie. The place, therefore, to locate teaching and judge its excellence or lack of excellence is in the student.

By shifting our viewpoint from that of the teacher acting to the student learning we shall be more accurately talking about teaching. At the same time we shall see better the distinction between the knowledge possessed and the conditions of its possession by the student. Not so obviously, but vital to our present problem, this viewpoint leaves no place for distinguishing the various sorts of ends when one is no longer expressly considering the agent—the college and the teacher. The only relevant distinction applicable to learning from a teacher is that between the knowledge that is acquired and the conditions or circumstances under which this acquired knowledge exists in the student's mind.

Knowledge and its state
by possession

From this viewpoint the proposition of this book can be more accurately stated. The Catholic college student acquires (or can acquire) from his being taught in school both knowledge and the state of its possession. Two elements of the student's learning need consideration. One is the knowledge;[6] the other is the state of its possession.

CHAPTER 4

KNOWLEDGE

AND LEARNING

FROM A TEACHER

In the last chapter we tried to establish the difference between knowledge gained and the state of its possession by the learner. Now we must look closer at knowledge. First we need to understand why knowledge can be got at all from a teacher. Common sense seems to back the statement that knowledge is related to learning in a way that moral virtue is not. Can this commonsense judgment be grounded firmly in the nature of knowledge and the activity of teaching-learning? To answer this question requires a consideration of knowing and learning from a teacher. And since our interest in the question is limited mainly to what is learned in college, some qualification must be put on the general data of knowledge and learning. That is, we need to indicate the kind of knowledge proper to college learning. This last need can best be answered by dividing knowledge in order to indicate which kind we are talking about. First, we shall divide knowledge and indicate the kinds acquired in college; second, we shall consider the nature of knowledge and of the act of learning from a teacher.

Knowledge can be divided in many ways. One division is between sense knowledge and intellectual knowledge. This division is especially pertinent when one is asking if men differ from animals. In all other considerations it invites one to think that an adult has some knowledge that is purely intellectual and some that is purely sensible. Experience will not bear this out. Some knowledge is more sensible, some more intellectual; but none is purely either. Another division, one that we explained above, is between speculative and practical knowledge. This division is always valid, though not too helpful in our present question. Liberal arts students concern themselves with both practical and speculative knowledge, though more with speculative than practical. Our consideration should keep these facts in mind, but it need not be controlled by this distinction. Another division, taking knowledge in its formed

state perfecting the human mind, is between the intellectual virtues of insight, science, wisdom, art, and prudence.
This division does not fit too well a discussion of learning
and teaching, since a man does not learn intellectual virtues nor does a teacher teach them. By learning he acquires the intellectual virtues but he does not learn them.
It would seem better when discussing knowledge gained
in school to divide knowledge in some genetic framework.
Our school system indicates that the student's knowledge
grows, from grammar school through graduate school,
both in extent and in depth. The student learns about
more things. Especially, he learns about the same things
in a better way. And this latter, rather than the former,
seems to be the ideal of the American liberal arts college.
If the way the student knows is more important than what
he knows—although this position can be pushed to absurdity[1]—it makes sense in our present consideration to divide
knowledge according to the way knowledge progresses.

Knowledge, as we said above, is the proper account of
something. To give such accounts is natural to man. By
that I mean that man likes to use his mind on the data of
his experience. Sometimes man wants knowledge because
it is needed to get action going. Sometimes, too, man
wants knowledge just to know. Witness the number and
persistence of sidewalk engineers at any construction site.
Man especially wants to know about himself and his actions as well as about the actions of other things. This, of
course, is only to say that man is rational, that he needs to
make his own life and actions intelligible to himself and,
on occasion, to others. The raw material of this rational
life is the varied experience he has of himself and of the
world around him.

Perfect human knowledge does not arise full-blown in one swift act that leaps from not knowing to knowing. Rather, as St. Thomas Aquinas points out,[2] we progress in knowledge by two lines of action. One consists in going from the more common to the less common; that is, to the more specific and precise. Suppose, for example, that a man looks down the street in the dusk of the evening and sees something in the street. He cannot quite make out what it is. He moves closer and sees that it is an automobile. Finally he gets close enough to determine the make and the model of that make. His knowledge goes from the vague to the precise. And if *dusk* and *move closer* are taken as metaphors, this example describes one movement towards improved knowledge. The second movement, parallel to the first, is from the knowledge that a thing is to the knowledge of what it is. Since "what a thing is" always means of what sort it is, this movement is from singular to universal knowledge. In the example above, the model of a certain make answered of what sort the individual was. Another example, I take from personal history. A young girl of five lived across the street from a home where seven priests lived. She knew one quite well, a Father Paul Smith, who was hardly five feet, five inches tall. One day, as she played in her yard, she saw a tall priest leave the house. She exclaimed to herself, "There is a tall Father Smith." The little girl was off in her wording; she was not off in her thinking. She saw quite well that to grasp an individual means to know what sort it is. And she succeeded, in spite of the easily remedied error in words, in making progress in knowledge. Such progression, from the vague to the precise, is the history of all human knowledge. But not all human knowledge progresses as far as knowledge can go. Consequently there is place for distinguishing knowledge according to stages or levels to which progress has been made. Such is our distinction between spontaneous knowledge, elaborated knowledge, and scientific knowledge.[3]

The first stage in the progress of knowledge is that of spontaneous knowledge. It results from man's attempt to find some sense in the confusing variety of human experiences. All sorts of experiences crowd into human consciousness. With the aid of memory, which can bring back past experiences, man finds, or is helped by others to find, similarities and distinguishing characteristics among past and present experiences. These discoveries of reason stand as islets of stability in the stream of experience.[4] Thus a man knows, for example, that men are different from animals or that heavy bodies fall faster than light ones or that if he wants something changed he had better do something about it. These spontaneous acts of knowledge grasp the intelligible factors in experience. What they do not grasp clearly is the reason or cause why this or that is so. Relying purely on such knowledge, a man might say that men are not animals because men are responsible for their actions whereas animals are not. But if one asks him what responsibility shows about human nature, he might be at a loss to do more than say that responsibility shows that man is not an animal; that is, he would say what he has already said.

Notice that spontaneous human knowledge may be quite as sound as knowledge ever will be. Yet its weakness, as knowledge, is that it is strictly unexamined. There is no sustained attempt to justify the truth of this knowledge or to purge it of possible misconceptions and error.

The facts of experience are taken on their face value and left imbedded in the sensible imagery that normal experience supplies. The acts of the mind ordering these experiential data are not examined for accuracy. Data, reasons, and conclusions are held in one undistinguished unity. Still, this lack of reflection and precision does not necessarily render spontaneous knowledge doubtful or untrue. The failure to reflect does, however, leave man open to the natural temptation to generalize too quickly. In the example above concerning falling bodies, one easily identifies more weight with greater speed of fall, owing to the images we have from daily life where lead is heavy and falls fast, and feathers are light and fall slowly. Relying on such images one easily concludes that the speed of fall depends on weight—a too quick generalization of spontaneous knowledge. The data here need to be examined and purified. The presence of air friction must be seen as part of the data, even though man does not experience this friction except in extraordinary circumstances. Spontaneous knowledge, with no tools to purify the data, is open to misconceptions and error whenever normal experience leaves a critical part of the data hidden.[5]

There is a second weakness in spontaneous understanding. This knowledge comes to be from immediate experience and is dependent on this source for its strength and vitality. A man alone in the open country during a violent thunderstorm begins to understand very forcefully his own insufficiency. He realizes there must be one who is sufficient, realizes that God exists. Now this spontaneous reasoning has all that any proof of God's existence needs, even though the acts and reasoning process are rough and ready. What such reasoning lacks is stability. For when the storm is over and our man is safe at home, the knowledge of God's existence is no longer so clear and persuasive because the sensible experience that gave rise to the knowledge is no longer exerting its influence on the mind. The man's conviction of God's existence is tied to a definite sensible experience. When that is no longer present in all its persuasive power, the conviction loses some of its certainty. Moreover, such knowledge, held in memory, is not easily communicable because the strength of the immediate experience is not easily communicable to one who is not undergoing this identical experience. What is needed to make this knowledge stable and more communicable is reflection. Not that reflection would make it more true. All that reflection can do is certify the truth that is present. Reflection would bring out more clearly the precise grounds of the conviction of God's existence and help one see that these grounds are not only present in the thunderstorm but in every experience man has of changing things. Reflection would also point up the reasonableness of the acts of the mind through which such knowledge is attained. Without such reflection, spontaneous knowledge lacks the means to notarize the truth that it possesses.

The second stage of progress in knowledge is that of elaborated knowledge. This can take either of two distinct paths. One is the artistic, the other is the reflective. Both are explanatory because they give a reason for what is. They differ in the ways they explain. Artistic knowledge explains by forming a new concrete whole or being. Reflective knowledge explains by separating and isolating the critical factors of the whole or of the being experienced. A word about each of these kinds of knowledge.

Artistic knowledge explains by constructing a singular. The art product, the constructed singular, is in a sense the artist's explanation, though the opposite of the kind of explanation an art critic would give of the art product. For the artist does not tell us about something; rather he presents his product as what he has to say. His "saying" is achieved by articulating the singular in such a way that the most significant intelligible factors shine through in a way easy and delightful to grasp. What the artist sees by a direct and unanalyzed insight he lays out (explains) in this matter or in this sensible imagery. If you asked a painter to explain his canvas, he would be perfectly justified in saying, "This picture is my explanation. I explain with color and line, for these are my language. What I have to say, my picture says." Thus the singular he constructs is his explanation, his expressed vision, alive with all the connotations and nuances and overtones that accompany concrete, singular things. Herein lies its proper power to make something plain. For it concentrates on the intelligible without sacrificing the prodigal complexity of the things we encounter. Herein, also, lies its peculiar human quality. For such explanation engages the whole man —mind, will, emotions, and body. Hence artistic knowledge is able to satisfy men's desire to know and can be the basis of noble human life. It is also a final human development in one way of knowing, since artistic knowledge leads to no knowledge beyond itself, except to more or better artistic knowledge.

As excellent as artistic knowledge is, it is not the only kind of knowledge open to man. Its very excellence, in fact, indicates its limitation. There are advantages to keeping intelligible factors situated in full-bodied reality, where the rich clarity of the individual is present. But the very richness of such clarity may be a disadvantage when man wants to see in detail the parts or elements which constitute the whole. The clarity emphasizing the elements must be attained by breaking down the whole. Thus detailed accuracy and precision in relation to constituent parts must be attained by reflection and analysis rather than by construction.

Before we turn to reflective knowledge something must be said, by way of parenthesis, about the knowledge of one contemplating a work of art. Such knowledge is not artistic because it does not make anything. It is speculative. Of course, this does not mean that literary criticism, for instance, has no role to play in the development of literary productions by poets and novelists and dramatists. But whatever its role, such knowledge is still speculative. Its object is what is, not what is to be made. It does not construct; it analyzes. Thus, in our division, it properly fits in with reflective knowledge, which we shall consider next. But it needs no special treatment there. Like all reflective knowledge, it can be done at two stages, that of elaborative and scientific reflection. Literary criticism is carried on at both levels. If nothing else, this fact would indicate that it is not artistic knowledge. We can, therefore, close the parenthesis and turn to reflective knowledge.

The reflective path of elaborating knowledge is by way of analysis, not by constructing a singular. It separates out the various intelligible factors of a given concrete whole. Some factors are seen to be essential, say, that a man is rational and free; some factors are accidental and relatively insignificant, say, that he is unshaved or skinny. The reflective movement consists in separating the insignificant from the essential in order to grasp the given at its core. In some data the core will be the universal of which the given particular is an embodiment. In other data the core will be the cause of the given effect. In yet other data the core will be the existence of a cause demanded by the existence of these data. The success of this reflective movement of the mind will, of course, depend on the reflective tools used.

The reflection being considered here, that of elaborated knowledge, uses the tools natural to man. By *natural* is meant those means of knowing that man has by his native endowment of reason and develops in the ordinary actions of living. These tools are observation, natural logic, and rhetoric.[6] Universals, principles, causes known through such tools, will be steeped in sensible imagery and therefore confined in their full meaning and applicability. For example, elaborated knowledge understands that man is a cultural being because he is a toolmaker and a creator of conceptual language. Both of these causes—making a tool and speaking words—are easily imaginable. But if one gave as the cause of man's openness to culture that he has immanent spiritual actions of thought and volition, the tools of elaborated knowledge would not be up to grasping causes so delineated. Again, elaborated knowledge can understand the constitution of the atom when it is presented in an imaginable model, with a number of small red and white balls circling around a central unit, much like the product of an erector set. (Spontaneous understanding would find it difficult to think that a material thing has space between its particles.) But the same knowledge of the atom presented in the form of mathematical equations, parts of which are not easily imaginable and parts of which cannot be imagined, would not be fully intelligible to a mind capable only of reflective elaborated knowledge. The weakness of elaborated knowledge is its concern with the imaginable. This is also its strength.

For elaborated knowledge is not constricted to one limited aspect of reality, as we shall see that scientific knowledge is. Its very generality is its excellence.[7] Because it concerns itself with those aspects of reality that are imaginable, it can range over all data that can be held by images. All it needs is a reason to ground its conclusions. Thus elaborated knowledge finds no embarrassment at gathering its food from the data of science or philosophy or literature or history, for it can find and substitute images for all such data. It can therefore share, in a limited way of course, in all specialized fields and make its possessor intelligent in many fields though a specialist in none. Also, it can protect a mind against the kind of intellectual imperialism that high specialization encourages. For when a man becomes expert in one kind of specialized knowledge, his way of knowing becomes so habitual and transparent to him, and the way others know so strange and opaque, that he may conclude others do not know because they do not know as he does.

This temptation to make all good knowledge be one kind of knowledge plagues all specialists, though it seems that the sciences are more likely to lead a man down this road than are the arts. But the error does not consist in this, that some natural science is set up as emperor of the mind. Whether it is a natural science or philosophy or mathematics or a social science or one of the arts, the harm to the mind is the same, for it substitutes a part for the whole. Elaborated knowledge makes it possible to keep some view of the whole. It can also make possible the beginnings of communication between specialists themselves and keep the isolating boundaries from becoming iron curtains.

Each type of elaborated knowledge, artistic and reflective, has its own peculiar excellence. Artistic knowledge is most fully human and is top in its line of knowledge, as we said before. Reflective knowledge, however, is not at its peak in the elaborated stage. In fact, its excellence is precisely that it prepares for something beyond itself. For the reflective process that refines images also prepares the mind to see the inadequacy of these images and of the refining tools that used such images. It thereby invites the mind to improve both tools and insights, making possible a more perfect form of reflective knowledge, that of scientific knowledge.

This last point needs exemplification. I shall take a case from the history of thought. William Paley, an eighteenth-century Anglican divine, thought that nature showed forth the existence of God. Being a thorough man, he brought together a prodigious array of natural observations, representing most of the "scientifically established facts" of his day.[8] He then argued with admirable rhetorical skill that just as a watchmaker is needed to explain a watch found on the moor, so there must be a great World-Maker to explain the immensely complicated world we find around us. The watch we see demands, because of its complicated structure, a watchmaker we do not see. How much more does the material world, far more complicated than a watch, demand a World-Maker! Notice that the argument proceeds from the complication of the arrangement of parts, which are parts by design, not by nature.

Such complication demands no more than a builder. Moreover, such complication does not demand the present existence of the builder but only existence at the moment of making. A watch found today does not guarantee the present existence of the watchmaker, only that he did exist; he could now be dead. Obviously, a God who once existed as architect and need not now exist is not the God of Christian revelation, who is Creator and necessarily exists. Paley's "proof," relying on natural (not specialized) tools and clearly inadequate, invites the Christian to look for a more adequate proof. In order to find such proof he will have to purify the experiential data beyond the level of complication of parts; he will have to examine closer the role of intellect in making; he will have to check his reasoning to see that the conclusion holds no more than the premises guarantee. He will, in short, have to do a better job of reflective thinking. This better job will be scientific knowing.[9]

Scientific knowledge is the third stage of progress in knowledge. It can be defined as certain knowledge through causes. The critical part of this definition is "certain knowledge." That is, the certainty must arise from the very explanatory value of the causes, which are seen to be such that it is impossible (and therefore unthinkable) for a thing to be or be such as it is unless it is this or unless these are its antecedents. This factor of necessity in scientific knowledge needs to be stressed, since this is its distinguishing mark. Sometimes one hears it said that scientists waste time proving what people have always known. Generally, "what people have always known" means spontaneous knowledge. To know the same truth now scientifically is an important advance in knowledge.

For a truth known as necessarily true is more truth, seeing that truth is the known conformity of mind with reality. If a thing must be or must be as it is, then the mind knowing that necessity is more conformed to what is than one that only knows that such is true but misses its necessity. Examples of this better knowing are mathematical demonstrations, the laws of motion for material reality, and the existence of God from the fact of existents unable to account for their own existence.

The proper mark of scientific knowledge is that it is reflective to the highest degree. Its tools are precise determination of the facts, rigorous logic, and nonfigurative and unequivocal expression. The whole thrust of this knowledge is to consider some precise and clearly distinguished aspect of the object and locate its cause exactly. The purpose in developing its highly specialized tools is to make possible a consciously reasonable check of all the factors of knowledge. Experience is not left vague but is manipulated until the sole factor to be considered is distinguished and isolated. The steps of reason working on such data are constantly checked by rules evolved by reason itself to insure reliable thinking about such data. Finally, the expression of such thinking must be unequivocal in order to exclude the possibility of two meanings to one statement and must be nonfigurative in order to exclude the possible confusion of the appearances of the data with the factors truly present in the data. With such tools both data and principles are constantly checked, and their use insures the certainty and necessity of the cause-effect relationship that constitutes this kind of knowing.

The excellence of scientific knowledge, as different from elaborated knowledge, is its precision. It goes beyond the general in order to know better some limited aspect of the data. Thus scientific knowledges tend to separate from each other as the very price of their precision. There is no physics which is also philosophy, no philosophy which is also biology. From first to last these knowledges are different. The aspect of the data differs and consequently the tools and conclusions differ. The controlled observation of experiment is no tool for philosophy, since the facts of existence, which philosophy considers, are mostly in before the experiment ever begins. Differing in data, in tools, and in conclusions, scientific knowledges tend to separate and specialize and partialize;[10] and this specialization is an excellence proper to knowledge. For knowledge as knowledge is better for being more precise. Still, such knowledge is not an unmixed good for man; at least it was not for the founders of the American liberal arts colleges.

Using our division of knowledge into spontaneous, elaborated, and scientific, we can consider the kinds of knowledges taught in a liberal arts college. First of all, spontaneous knowledge contains some truths not teachable at all; for example, the knowledge of first principles, such as, "What is, is; and what is cannot simultaneously not be." Without such knowledge teaching is impossible.[11] Beyond these basic truths, spontaneous knowledge is primarily the work of grammar-school teaching, even though no period of adult life excludes such knowing. In general, the high school concentrates on elaborated knowledge of both the artistic and reflective type. The liberal arts college continues and deepens elaborated knowledge, and lays the foundation for scientific knowledge. The graduate school concentrates on perfecting scientific knowledge, and treats artistic knowledge as scientifically as possible.

This partitioning of knowledges throughout the school system is intended to be, and is, only roughly accurate. The progress in knowledge, like all other living actions, is not separable into precise stages where one ends and the other begins at a perfectly defined point. The knowledge learned in the last years of grammar school is very close to that learned in the first years of high school, and the same is true of the last years of high school and the first year of college. In spite of this overlapping, we can still say that the knowledges taught in the American liberal arts college are elaborated and scientific knowledges.

Recall that elaborated knowledge includes both artistic and reflective. Artistic knowledge, in the setting of teaching and learning, must itself be distinguished into the knowledge of the rules of an art and the knowledge directing actual making. The knowledge of the rules of an art grounds both the ability to appreciate a work of art and to execute works of art. But such knowledge is not of itself sufficient for either appreciation or production. Both these latter require a judgment about the proper application of the rules of an art in this concrete instance. In learning from works of art, this judgment is called good taste; in producing works of art, this judgment is the art of the artist. Neither judgment is fully teachable. The part of it that is teachable is the rules or canons of the art. Thus a college emphasizes the rules of the arts as that part of artistic knowledge most teachable. It uses what means it can, mainly doing actions, to encourage both good taste and artistic production. But it can expect of students at least the knowledge of the rules of the arts it teaches.[12]

Reflective knowledge has a lower place in college than artistic because reflective knowledge is only preparatory and substitutional. It prepares the student to move into scientific knowledge. Having thought about certain data as expressed and ordered by natural tools, the student is ready to improve his reflective knowledge by using precise scientific tools on the same data. Where the facts were expressed in images, they are now expressed in concepts that may or may not be imagined. And these concepts should be seen precisely as perfecting the former knowledge. In fact, this is the art of teaching introductory courses in scientific knowledge. Teaching should start with the data as reflective knowledge handles them and show the inadequacies of such knowledge. The cure for such inadequacies is then seen to be the scientific knowledge the student is beginning.

Reflective knowledge also has a substitutive value in liberal arts colleges. As was said above, scientific knowledge is specialized and exclusive. A man may be expert in one field of such knowledge and have no comparable knowledge in any other field. He is thereby a limited knower and also a limited man. Yet, what is he to do? To improve reflective knowledge is to raise it to scientific knowledge. He cannot refuse improvement in his knowledge. Such improvement, however, condemns him to partialization because only the most gifted can become truly competent in more than one scientific field. The way out of this problem is to keep conversant with other scientific knowledges by means of sophisticated reflective knowledge. Hence its substitutive value. This reflective knowledge can never fill the shoes of scientific knowledge. It can, though, serve as an inferior substitute for the scientific knowledges one does not have the time or native talent to acquire.

Of course, sophisticated reflective knowledge is no sufficient ideal for a liberal arts college of today. Its excellence
is not great enough. But when it is joined with the truly
excellent in one field it can stand as the lesser but essential
part of the liberal arts ideal. For it serves the purpose of
moderating the inherent tendency of specialization to nar-
row its possessor and to isolate him from other knowledges
and other men.

Little need be said about scientific knowledge. By indi-
rection we have already given it a top place, along with
artistic knowledge, in the liberal arts colleges. Generally,
too, it receives more attention than artistic knowledge.
One reason for this is its possibility of being turned to
some professional end. Another is that it is more teachable
than artistic knowledge. This last reason needs clarification. To speak of knowledge as more or less teachable requires that one be clear about what makes knowledge
teachable. This, recall, was the second step proposed for
this chapter.

Speculative knowledge deals with facts. This might
mean only that knowledge is about facts, as if facts were
simply the condition of knowledge, much as clothes are
the condition of being clothed. Facts are much more than
conditions; they are the first principle of knowledge, as
we said above. Facts cause knowledge, and nothing else
will cause it. For knowledge is a qualification of the
knower in terms of the known. Given a being, it can act
on the knowing powers to specify them. The mind, specified by the thing, is a knowing mind. If there is no one
thing to do the specifying, there is no specification; that
is, no knowledge. The knowledge of absolute nothing
would itself be nothing.[13] All of this means simply that

facts talk to our minds and that nothing else really does. Even when men talk to us, it is the facts that talk through them.[14] That is why we understand nothing when a man speaks a language we do not know. His sounds we know; what we do not know are the facts his sounds refer to. His words are noises to us, not intelligible language. Intelligible language is speech that tells us about facts or what are proposed as facts. When we know the facts are talking through another, we understand both that he speaks for the facts and what the facts are he speaks for. When we do not know whether or not the facts speak through him, we know only that he speaks—that is a fact—but we do not know from him what the facts are.

Facts, as I have been using the term, are not things; rather they are aspects of things. Any one thing grounds many facts. This book, for example, is made of paper and cloth and ink, plus some thread and glue; its pages are a fixed size; it is philosophical; it is an essay; it deals with education; it treats of moral virtue and knowledge; it is copyrighted; it is the publisher's to reprint; it is yours to resell but not to reprint; and so on. The "and so on" does not mean that the facts this one book presents have been pretty well exhausted. It means the opposite, that since no one is likely to finish listing all the facts about this book, there is no point in continuing beyond the spot where it is seen that such a list would be endless. Thus facts are not just things. The number of facts is always greater than the number of things. Facts are the aspects of things, the things as presented to a knowing power.

In some discussions, facts can be used as the equivalent of things. The reason for this is that since we know things through their facts, we can in some considerations substitute one for the other without causing confusion. Here, however, where the question is the nature of a fact, such substitution will not do. One thing yields endless facts because one thing has many facets or aspects presentable to a knowing power. And the order is not that first one knows the thing and then some facet or aspect of it. The order is the other way. It is by knowing an aspect that one knows the thing. Take a tuning fork that has been struck lightly. Its production of sound waves is one aspect of the tuning fork, one presentable only to the sense of hearing. If a man had only one sense, that of hearing, he would know only a sounding thing. And if this thing (tuning fork) were not producing sound waves, he would not know it as thing, supposing that hearing is the only sense the man has. Thus for hearing, to be is to be sounding; to be sounding is to be, as far as hearing knowledge is concerned. This aspect of sounding is a fact to hearing; it is not a fact to sight. A fact is an aspect of a thing by which the thing is presentable to a knowing power.

All facts are, of course, objective. They must be, since they are aspects of things. But not all are objective in the same way. Some are objective and not repeatable; for example, that Caesar crossed the Rubicon. Some are objective and are repeatable; for example, that iron has an atomic weight of 55.8. Again, some facts are objective and are checkable by any capable person; for example, that heavy bodies do not fall faster than light ones. Some are objective but not checkable except by special persons; for example, that my mother loves me. Facts that are repeatable and checkable by any capable person are in a sense common facts. They are common to many things; they are also presentable to minds commonly. Facts that are not either repeatable or checkable are individual facts. They are neither common nor can they be commonly presented to minds, except on the word of another. Because tied to one thing, they exist here and now, in circumstances that are peculiar and private to this one thing.[15]

We began this discussion of the kinds of facts for the purpose of deciding whether one sort of knowledge is more teachable than another. Knowledge is about facts and different knowledges about different kinds of facts. From the side of knowledge, we have what is needed to approach our question. But the second factor, teaching, needs to be understood. So far we have said little about teaching beyond pointing out that it begins in the teacher and is completed in the student. It is time that we took a good look at what teaching is.

Our problem can be put in this way: What precisely does any teacher do when he is exercising his act of teaching? We shall not fall into the temptation of listing the desirable personal qualities a good teacher should have, such as being inspiring, sympathetic, enthusiastic, dramatic, and so on. All of these could equally well characterize a successful insurance salesman. If they did, they would not make him a teacher or even a salesman, though they would probably make him a better salesman. The same characteristics may make a teacher a better teacher; they will not of themselves make him a teacher. We are asking about the act that makes a teacher a teacher.

Also, for purposes of clarity, we shall not speak of teaching practical knowledge; that is, how to do or make.[16] We shall limit the discussion of teaching to teaching speculative knowledge. And we shall suppose that, although anyone can learn by himself, no one can teach himself. Thus our problem has the following data—a teacher possessing the knowledge; a student who does not possess the knowledge before being taught but only after having been taught. With these data before us, we ask: What is done when a teacher causes a student's knowledge?[17]

Now, any answer given to our question supposes some judgment about what it is to begin to know. Here is a student. Before he attended the class, he did not know; after the class he does know. How account for this new knowledge? There are two extreme answers to this question. You can say (*a*) that the "new" knowledge is not really new, that it was there all the time but the student was not aware of it; or (*b*) that it wasn't there in any sense but came to the student wholly from the outside, as coffee comes into a cup. Once either of these positions is taken, your explanation is pretty well determined in its main lines.

Take the first answer. It runs straight at the problem. The student does have the knowledge after having been taught; yet there is no way of explaining how he passed from not having it to having it. Therefore he must have had it all the time. But it seems that he begins to know. Then this "seeming" needs to be accounted for. Plato thought that minds lived in a former existence and there knew everything.[18] When they were put into the body, their knowledge was still present but obscured. By the proper questioning a mind could be stirred up to recall what it formerly knew. Plato even worked out an educational experiment on a slave boy to bolster his position.[19] Teaching, consequently, could be no more than encouraging a student to recall, even though it may "seem" that the teacher gives the student knowledge.

Contemporaries, too, hold this position. They would hardly, of course, talk of a preexistent mind; indeed they talk none too clearly even about mind, whether existent or preexistent. They do think, however, that to learn is to organize responses. As Dewey put it, "Speaking accurately, all direction is but *re*-direction; it shifts the activities already going on into another channel."[20] In other words, the difference between a student not knowing and knowing is only a difference between unorganized responses and organized ones. In any case the responses were there all the time; nothing new is added; the old is merely rearranged. And since rearranging is, according to Dewey, knowledge, knowledge was already in the student before it was taught. It needed only rearrangement. On this basis, teaching, now called progressive, is no more than encouraging a student to organize his own actual responses towards social utility.

The first answer, then, both ancient and contemporary, leaves very little for the teacher to do because no change really takes place. With nothing to do that is vital to the student's taught knowledge, the teacher bustles about the learner, opening windows, keeping records, planning better desks and plumbing. He arouses curiosity; he encourages; he comforts; he sets up circumstances that will call out this or that response. But he never gets into the student's act of learning. And his "causality" is completely external and purely dispositive. It no more accounts for the student's new knowledge than good health accounts for success in athletics or a traffic cop accounts for my driving downtown.

The second answer, exactly opposed to the first, says that learning is entirely from the outside. Here, too, the ancients hit the problem head on.[21] They maintained that since the student, before being taught, did not know and, after being taught, did know, knowledge must therefore have come from some outside source. Moreover, this outside source must be big enough to produce knowledge. No man is up to this. So, it takes a pure intellect that necessarily knows and consequently can send out this knowledge like rays from the sun. The student's job was to receive this knowledge; and whatever he did on his own was merely preparatory to his passive reception of this knowledge from the outside. Again, contemporaries duplicate the main lines of the ancients' answer. Without the attempted metaphysical justification of teaching but convinced nonetheless that knowledge is wholly from the outside, the moderns hit upon the teacher as the giver of knowledge. The teacher has knowledge; he passes it on by teaching; the student merely takes it from the teacher. Teaching then becomes the handing on of knowledge, quite as physical objects are handed on from one person to another.

Just as the first answer left little for the teacher to do, so this second answer leaves little for the student. According to the second answer, the student becomes a sort of sensitive sponge, receiving patiently and holding by memory what the teacher pours into or over him. With the student's role reduced to receiving and the teacher's function to giving, the question remains, Can the human teacher put knowledge into a student's mind like that? Were knowledge like marbles and the mind like a sack, it would be no trick to pass on knowledge. But the problem persists precisely because knowledge is not like marbles and minds are not like sacks. Even if they were, the account would not be satisfactory. For then a teacher who passed on knowledge would lose the knowledge he gave to the student; and, thus, to teach would be to talk oneself out of a job. Moreover, a student, according to that explanation, would never really possess knowledge, any more than the sack possesses the marbles put into it.

After rejecting both answers, we are now left with two negations on our hands. Our denial of the first answer leaves us with this proposition: Students do not have the knowledge they are taught before they are taught. And our denial of the second answer leaves us with this proposition: Students cannot be given knowledge by the teachers as they might be given candy bars. Neither proposition, considered singly, is too jarring. Take the beginner in physics. He does not know what mass is. Nor does the teacher pass him this knowledge as he does a blue book for a quiz; otherwise every student would know what mass is at the end of the period. Yet both statements, taken together, are very unintelligible. If the student does not somehow know what mass is before the class but does know it after, then his knowledge must have come from some source. Yet not, we agreed, from the student; he did not have it before the class. Nor can it, we agreed, come from a teacher handing it over to him; otherwise the teacher would be out his knowledge. Whence then is this new knowledge of mass?

It might look like a way out of the maze to say that the student does not have knowledge of mass but is in potency to it, much as cold water is in potency to heat. But this does not help much, because fire in the real sense gives heat to the water, even if it does not give away its heat to the water; but, according to our second proposition, the teacher neither gives nor gives away his knowledge to the student. This is to say that beginning to know is like—but not quite like—beginning to be hot. Knowing has its own difficulties, as Plato saw and stated clearly. Either we know what we are looking for, or we do not. If we know, there is no point in seeking; if we do not know, we can never tell when we find it.[22] There is no escaping this dilemma if knowing is like other changes.

The point is that the genesis of knowledge in a student is not quite like the genesis of heat in water. Nor is the potency to become hot quite like the potency to know. Cold water only receives heat; it cannot on its own become hot. But the student in potency to knowledge can know on his own. To know is at least to exercise one's own act. When a mind is presented with sensible reality and acts as a mind, the least we can say of it is that it knows; that is, it does the knowing. And this act of knowing is knowledge. Consequently, knowledge is not merely a perfection which is receivable; there is more to it than that. There is activity on the part of the student.

Moreover, this activity of the student is not active in the same way regarding all types of data. Some things the student understands without being taught; other things he sees in the light of untaught knowledge. For example, a child knows an apple first of all as something, and then, if he eats it, as something good to eat; or he knows the apple is red because he sees it is. But whether he knows the apple as edible or red, he could not know either unless he knew that apples are not not-apples, or that red is not not-red. If the principles of noncontradiction and identity were not present to his mind, he could never affirm with certainty, "The apple is red." For without these principles in his mind the red apple could just as well stand in his mind as not-apple and as not-red; he could affirm nothing because he would know nothing to affirm. In order to know anything beyond them, therefore, he must actually know being and its first principles. Such knowledge—that is, of being and its first principles—is untaught. It is acquired, yes; but not by being taught. It is another kind of knowledge that is taught, not the knowledge of the principles of being.

We are now in a position to clarify our propositions. The first one was that a student does not have knowledge before he is taught. This means that he does not know, before being taught, what he is taught. But he does know what he is not taught and what no one can teach him: being and its first principles. This knowledge was acquired without the aid of a teacher. This acquired but untaught knowledge is the solid ground from which both teaching and learning start. Now recall our second proposition, that a student cannot be given knowledge in the same way he can be given a blue book or in quite the same way that water is given heat. This does not mean, though, that his taught knowledge is not caused by the teacher. Consider the data. Both teacher and student have actual knowledge of first principles. Beyond that knowledge the teacher also has actual knowledge of their application, while the student has not. The teacher, by the arts of grammar and rhetoric, points out the lines from the facts to the principles, so that the facts are seen in the clear light of known principles. And the student, by following the teacher, also sees the lines connecting the facts to the already known principles and can then affirm this truth as seen by himself. This affirmation is his own act, not the teacher's; yet it is caused by the teacher's art at the same time that it is caused by the student.

Let us take a case of teaching something. To make it concrete let our task be to teach the Thomistic notion of potency. We are aware of the two pitfalls, (*a*) to think potency is nothing and (*b*) to think it is a shadowy something. We begin by saying potency is the ability to become. Very little progress here; nothing but blank stares from the class. We begin again, this time with a question. Does a brick know geometry? No. Can a brick ever know geometry? No. Can a baby? Yes. Then the lack of knowledge of geometry in a baby really means no actual knowledge of geometry but potential knowledge of geometry. Let us move on. This lack of knowledge of geometry in a baby, is it no knowledge of the first ten theorems or of the first two or of just a little bit of geometry, say, a postulate or two? It is no knowledge of geometry, not even of a postulate, any more than there is knowledge of geometry in a brick. But though neither actually knows geometry, a baby nevertheless can know it. Suppose we give a name to this lack of actual knowledge of geometry but potency to know. We shall call it potential knowledge of geometry. Then we can say that potency is not a something, not even a shadowy something; nor is it, indeed, simply nothing. It is between nothing and something, a nothing ordered to something.

What went on in this teaching of the notion of potency? First of all, the teacher knew what potency was. This knowledge he could have expressed clearly by talking about becoming, about the determinable principle of reality, about an *ens quo*. But he might well have been merely talking without teaching. He began to teach when he

talked about things the student had actual knowledge of
—bricks, babies, and geometry. Included in the student's
actual knowledge were the following propositions (lighted
by their principles), (*a*) that bricks are bricks and babies
babies (whatever is, is); (*b*) that babies can grow up and
learn (whatever is, can be); (*c*) that some people know
geometry (whatever is, is); (*d*) that bricks do not grow
up and never know geometry (what is not, is not).

Knowing these truths the student already knows cases
of potency, but he does not see what the cases involve;
that is, potency. Obviously, the art of the teacher consists
precisely in presenting these known facts in such a way
that the potency principle in these cases becomes present
in the mind of the student.

But this is no more than saying that the teacher teaches.
The question still remains, How does the teacher do this?
In other words, what is it to teach? To teach is to use
signs[23] of one's own knowledge, which knowledge is by
hypothesis knowledge of things. The student receives
these signs through his senses as signifying the teacher's
knowledge about things. Thus signs, through the medium
of knowledge, take the place of things they signify.[24] Playing the role of object (fact), they also exert the causality
of the object. For there is a line of causality from the real
to the intellect. In the face of the evidently real a thinking mind knows that reality. And though the mind is the
efficient cause of its own knowledge, the object nevertheless acts to specify what it is that is known. So also does
the object's substitute, the sign. The teacher's sign can,
however, have one advantage over the thing in nature.
For this natural thing exists under the conditions of matter and is therefore actually sensible and only potentially

intelligible. The teacher's words, on the other hand, are signs of his own knowledge, in which the fact is already actually intellectualized. So the student, through the teacher's words, is presented with a substitute object much closer to his own intellect and therefore more easily known than the raw, unprepared thing is.

But we have not yet come to the essential role of the teacher. Not only the teacher but the writer, too, presents knowledge through signs, and the reader learns from him. If the writer can do the teacher's work, why not get rid of the teachers and buy better texts? Teachers are of course got rid of, but others always take their places, no matter how good the texts are. The essential role of the teacher must be other than the writer's. And it is. Both present knowledge through signs. The writer, however, prepares one set of signs for imaginary readers and freezes his signs in type, while the living teacher, before living students, adapts his signs to fit the students before him. Blank stares, puzzled faces, pointless questions, all warn the teacher that he and his students are in the rough. The artist-teacher then varies his signs until those present get back on the fairway again. The role, therefore, essential to the teacher is to adapt signs so that the object or fact, present to the teacher's mind, becomes present to the living students before him. We might also say that the teacher, by adapting his signs, brings knowledge to students. Better still, he brings students to knowledge.

This analysis of the act of teaching makes clear two points, important for our subject. First, teaching as an action is achieved most fully in the student taught. Second, the result of successful teaching is the possession of a knowledge common to teacher and student. Both possess knowledge of the same facts. Moreover, both possess these facts in the same way, as being facts each one himself knows to be, although the student need not necessarily know with the same perfection the teacher does. One does not become a scholar in one day or one year. But if facts are held only by hearsay and memory—not known to be facts by the one knowing—one never becomes a scholar. Thus the individual possession of common facts possessed in a common way is the essential outcome of teaching.

This conclusion about teaching becomes the criterion for determining which facts are teachable, which more teachable. That is, facts are teachable to the extent that they can be commonly possessed. Teaching demands that the same facts be possessed by teacher and student in the same way. Common facts can be so possessed. By contrast, private facts may perhaps be possessed by two but never in the same way. Because of their individual and personal orientation such facts can be understood by one or another and held by all others only by hearsay (and memory); consequently, individual and personal facts cannot be taught in any accurate sense of the word.[25] Common facts are properly teachable facts. Our criterion can be put negatively. The more individual and personal and private the facts are the less teachable they are. This form of our principle will help us decide which knowledges are less teachable, which more.

We are in a position now to see why scientific knowledge is more teachable than artistic knowledge, more teachable than any other. It deals with facts which already are; and of those, it concentrates on common facts. Common facts, as we said above, are those which are repeatable and checkable. As repeatable, common facts are easily presentable by teacher to student. If any one of them is successfully presented and clearly known, all of its cases, actual and possible, are also known in this one case of the common. The student who sees what mass is in iron knows what mass is in any material substance. Such a fact is also checkable by the student. He can see for himself that the teacher's words precisely report and order facts open to his own discovery. Thus the student can easily posssess the same fact the teacher does and possess it in the same way. This is what we said constituted successful teaching.

Artistic knowledge, contrasted with scientific, differs all along the line. Its facts are not what are but what are to be made. What is, of course, is not makable. What could be is makable and is therefore open to artistic knowing, which proceeds by constructing and not by analysis. Nor can the makable be common, either from the side of the maker or the made. The maker, in order to get into action, must decide that it is good for him to make this fact (thing). Such a decision is a personal choice, private and peculiar to this one individual maker. The thing made must also be individual, since the common is not makable (imagine making a universal pie that is at once all flavors and all kinds!). Finally, the art-made fact (thing) is not fully checkable by any capable person. There is no other exactly like it to check with. A kind of check is possible for some of the factors employed in making. The material used, for instance, will be the basis of some checkable aspects. Paint and stone have their own proper conditions for being manipulated in making. Also, what is made has conditions of its own. A statue of Lincoln will, for example, have to be in some sense like Lincoln. Both

of these aspects, the material used and the kind of thing
made, are general and therefore in a sense checkable. Yet
these alone are not the most decisive factors of making.
Most critical is the idea the maker is trying to embody.
Only the maker can know this fully; he alone can check,
in the fullest sense, product against idea. It is true, the
general norms for working in this or that material can be
made common and taught, but the exact application of
such norms to this one product cannot be generalized.
Here the individual must act on his own, so that he rather
learns by doing than by being taught.

If we consider the speculative knowing of the products
of art, the situation is changed somewhat. Here there are
facts that are—art objects such as paintings, plays, novels.
The things exist and are there to be known. The mind
considering such art products will try to find what common facts are present in such data; for example, how this
product fits the general norms of making in this material;
how the thing made fits as a case of a certain kind. But
the mind never finds a common fact at the core of the art
product. The reason is that the central fact of an art product, the personal vision of the artist, can never be univer-
salized without destroying it. Nor can an art object be
checked by another exactly like it, since there is none like
it.[26] However, merely because the art object cannot be
treated as other things can, this does not mean that art
objects are incapable either of expanding knowledge or
being checkable. For example, Macbeth is an individual
man who could be, and there is no other exactly like him.
Yet in knowing Macbeth, any man can know himself—and
all men—by finding in himself or others some of what
made Macbeth be Macbeth. And such knowledge, check-

able in its own fashion, can be gained in all its concrete strength and forcefulness only by keeping Macbeth his individual self.

Thus art objects can be taught as to their common aspects, say, the canons of the drama. Such facts, being common, are relatively easy to teach. But the insight that is at the heart of the art object is much more difficult to teach. Its individual character might exclude teaching altogether, were it not for the fact that such insights are checkable in one's own private experience of an insight in some sense approaching, though possibly never reproducing exactly, what the artist put into his work. The fact that the artist's individual vision, at least in any great work of art, is shareable by any capable person makes it teachable to a certain extent, though not easily so. For teaching of this sort, however, a man needs the art of teaching in a high degree.

Our principle of teachability—that private facts, especially those consequent on choices, are not teachable—will help us understand why moral virtues are not strictly teachable and why some intellectual virtues are more teachable than others. Moral virtues cannot be learned from a teacher because moral virtue requires decision and choices. However, the part of moral virtue that consists in the knowledge of what sort of actions are virtuous can be taught. This knowledge deals with facts that are common to all men. But such knowledge is not moral virtue but only the knowledge of its norms. The supernatural virtues, which are gifts of God, cannot be learned from a teacher, except the knowledge part of the virtue of faith. The part that requires preference or choice is not teachable. Intellectual virtues, considered as virtue, cannot be learned from a teacher. An intellectual virtue is the acquired modification of the intellect by which it becomes constantly ready to consider facts of a certain kind with ease and accuracy. Ease and accuracy in thinking are purely personal and not transferable. What the mind feeds on and what makes it ready and accurate, however, are facts; and these are teachable. Thus the intellectual virtues considered as knowledge of facts can be learned from a teacher.

Some intellectual virtues, considered as knowledge of fact, are less learnable from a teacher than others, depending on the presence of preference or choice in such knowledge. The intellectual virtue of art we considered just now. The virtue of prudence deals with what one person should do here and now, and is therefore eminently personal and never common. What I should do may differ from what you should do in the same external circumstances. Preference enters such knowledge in order to see what is good for me here and now. The virtue of wisdom, also, which orders all things to the ultimate end, includes the factor of good will. The virtue of intelligence or insight is the clear knowledge of first principles. This knowledge is partly natural and partly acquired by activity. The part that is acquired—that is, the knowledge of how the first principles pervade all reality—can be learned from a teacher. The natural part is not learnable from a teacher, for it is supposed in all teaching. The only intellectual virtue left is that of science, which is certain knowledge through causes. Since there is no preferential factor present in this knowledge and all of it deals with common facts, the virtue of science is eminently learnable from a teacher. For that reason we shall emphasize the acquiring of scientific knowledge, seeing that this is the privileged case of teaching-learning. And since scientific knowledge can be gained only after much preparation, we shall include getting this preparatory sort of knowledge, which we called elaborated knowledge.

The eminent teachability of scientific knowledge justifies our emphasis upon such knowledge. This, of course, is the main reason for the emphasis. Certainly the knowledge of the arts as well as knowledge of art objects plays an equally important role in the liberal arts college. Yet these are not as teachable as scientific knowledge is, where learning from a teacher can be seen in its simplest form. Moreover, by the very fact that such knowledge has no factor of choice or preference, there is less likelihood that we will prejudice the outcome in our own favor. In an inquiry about the presence of moral influences in learning by being taught, to concentrate on knowledge that has within it the factor of choice is in some sense to load one side of the scale. It seems better to see what the case is for moral virtue in the acquisition of knowledge that has within it no preferential factors whatever. For example, does the learning of mathematics from a teacher leave any place for acts of choice? Can six and five be twelve, if I so prefer? Or will the reasoned assents of mathematics be absolutely impervious to preference? Where there is no act of choice, there is no question of moral virtue.

At this point it is essential to recall that the reasoned assents of scientific knowledge are speculative assents. That is, the mind knows what the facts are. It assents that so and so is true because the mind sees that the facts are and must be as they are. Nothing more is needed for such assents; nothing less will be sufficient. To let anything come between facts and speculative knowledge of them is to block all assent. A denial of this proposition is a denial that speculative knowledge is knowledge. For speculative knowledge is so related to facts that if it is not about facts, real or supposed, it does not exist at all. Its whole being, as we said above, is to be about. Knowledge is good when it represents what the facts are. Knowledge is bad when some "fact" which is not is represented as if it were, or when some fact that is, is represented as if it were not. In either case speculative assents are controlled and specified by the facts.[27] Every phase of the interior act of reasoned assent follows the demands of the facts. The principles used must arise from the understanding of the kind of facts being considered.[28] The problem to be solved must be one that is resident in such facts. The conclusion or reasoned assent must be verified of such facts. The surest way to block reasoned assent is to get away from the kind of facts under consideration.

Try, for instance, to scramble the chemical and economic facts about gold. That gold has an atomic weight of 197.2, a specific gravity of 19.3, and is the most malleable of all metals has nothing to do at all with its being a medium of exchange. That it is a scarce metal, and thus can serve as an exchange medium, has nothing whatever to do with its being the most ductile of all metals. The problems that gold raises for a chemist would be meaningless to an economist, just as the problem of the gold standard, which fascinates the economist, has no relevance for a chemist. Finally, the principles which the economist uses to resolve his problem would be worthless in the work of the chemist trying to solve his.

The point here is not merely that knowledge in all its stages is bound to facts but that it is so bound to its own facts that nothing, not even other facts about the same thing, can come between problem-principle-conclusion and the proper facts supporting such knowledge.

This tight union of knowledge with its own facts is the essential condition of reasoned assents. What place can there be, then, for moral factors to intrude? And if they do, what other effect can they have except to hinder or block assent? Moral or religious factors have no relevance to mathematics or physics. To talk about Christian mathematics and Christian physics would seem to be talking nonsense. As reasoned assents, knowledges of these sciences are tied to facts—the same for Christians and non-Christians—so closely that the knowledges must follow the demands of these facts at the price of not being reasoned assents when separated from them. Analytic geometry is the same, as reasoned assents, no matter who teaches it or to whom it is taught. And the same is true of history and sociology and philosophy. Among philosophers, both those in a Catholic college and those in a non-Catholic college, there may be disagreement about principles and conclusions; and there may even be disagreement about what the facts are. But there is no disagreement about this, that philosophy to remain philosophy must be tied to its facts, if there are reasoned scientific assents called philosophical. And those who think there is no philosophy think so because they think there are no facts for philosophy to be about.[29] Knowledge by its nature is a specification of the knower in terms of the object's (fact's) specification.

Having said this about the nature of reasoned assents, we must immediately add, "However." But the "however" is not introduced in order to take back with the left hand what the right hand has given. What has been given, stands. One does not tamper with essences or natures, unless he is willing to confuse himself as well as others. And if the only object under discussion at present were the nature of reasoned assents, there would be nothing more to say. But our object is a student's learning from a teacher by making reasoned assents. These, students and teachers, are living and acting in conditions set up and maintained by their own history and choices. No data presented by the teacher and no assent made by the students take place in an intellectual and moral vacuum. Assents are made by persons with minds already holding other assents and wills already committed to this or that good. Thus new assents come into a room already partly furnished and must find a fitting place in that room.

The relation of reasoned assents to conditions of their possession should not be misunderstood. Reasoned assents stand on their own feet, as we have indicated. They are neither made nor unmade by the conditions of their possession. Only known fact can make or unmake them. If the conditions of possession could rightfully substitute for fact, no reasoned assent would be worth the effort required to make it. But this excellence of reasoned assents need not blind us to the presence of other factors; in this case, to factors not controlled by the assents. The conditions of possession are outside and independent of the facts and principles that assents dominate. Hence, they have no right to decree under what conditions they will exist; that is, in the mind of a good or bad person, or in a mind with or without the faith.

One way to state the relation of assents to their concrete existential conditions is to say that such conditions are accidental to reasoned assents. The partial truth in this

statement is that assents, if considered as things in themselves (substances), can exist in these or other conditions
and in either case would be the same assent. But then, all
the other connotative meanings of "accidental" get into
the act. One is that the accidental is what is added to, or
happens to, a thing and could just as well not happen to it.
Some conditions do not happen to reasoned assents. If
anything, the reasoned assents "happen" to the conditions.
Some conditions (for example, the presence of faith in a
student's mind) are operative before the learning act
begins, and reasoned assents are brought in as the new
addition. *Accidental* may imply "nonimportant." Some
conditions of learning are of utmost importance in any college and very far from being accidental. In a Catholic
college they are so far from being accidental in this sense
that Catholics are willing to support two school systems
just to insure them. *Accidental* may also refer to whatever
flows from a thing as one of its perfections or accomplishments, such as the playing actions of a kitten. This meaning fits some conditions of learning no better than the
others did. Moral virtue and the faith are not the accomplishments of reasoned assents of scientific knowledge. If
anything, they are the accomplishments of free choices.
Finally, *accidental* may mean the opposite of substantial
without specifying the ground of opposition. But this
meaning is no more applicable than the others. There is
no opposition between reasoned assents and the conditions of their existence in a mind. If there were, it would
be impossible for there to be reasoned assents, as we said
above. Reasoned assents, in order to exist, must exist under
some conditions other than themselves. Were there opposition between the two, there could be no reasoned assents.

We have analyzed the nature of reasoned assents and concluded that they depend on facts and the principles proper to such facts and depend in principle on nothing else. We have indicated that among the reasoned assents some are eminently teachable—scientific facts—because they are common to all minds. Facts are less teachable when they cannot be common either because the facts are not open to all or are dependent in some fashion on preference. Thus the most teachable knowledge among the subjects taken in a liberal arts college is the scientific knowledges. As to elaborated knowledges, the reflective sort is more easily taught than the artistic. In the arts the normative and canonical is more teachable than the exercise of the art. In all teaching the norm is the commonness of fact and principle and therefore the possible commonness to teacher and student of the assent made to such facts.

CHAPTER 5

EXISTENTIAL CONDITIONS

OF REASONED ASSENTS

IN A CATHOLIC COLLEGE

We distinguished, in Chapter 3, between knowledge and the state of its possession. Knowledge, considered in the framework of learning from a teacher, is an assent made to facts presented by a teacher. The state of possession of knowledge, in the same framework of learning from a teacher, will become the existential conditions under which student assents are made. To list all such conditions, besides being impossible, is outside the purpose or demands of our present discussion. Our interest is limited to those that have some relevance to the moral virtue of the student. Moreover, among the morally operative existential conditions of reasoned assents, we shall consider those most operative in a Catholic college. Hence the rather wordy title of this chapter.

To limit our field to the existential conditions of assents made in Catholic colleges does not imply that there are not similar conditions in other colleges. Some treated in this chapter are present in any college. Some, of course, are peculiar to the Catholic college. And every college sets up existential conditions of learning, whether intending to do so or not. Even attempting to be morally neutral in teaching and learning is itself a condition. The reason is that assents made in a completely neutral moral atmosphere are subject to this existential condition just as much as those which are made in a moral setting. This point, the effect of moral existential conditions on reasoned assents, will constitute the matter of the present chapter. We shall consider such conditions under the following heads: those arising from the learner; those arising from the teacher; those arising from the faith, a condition common to both teacher and learner.[1]

First, then, the existential conditions arising from the learner. The most obvious of these is the knowledge already present in the student's mind. What he has learned from his experience in living and learning stands as the existing framework into which new knowledge must come.

A student, for instance, with a strong background of natural science will tend to make all new knowledge fit into the patterns most familiar to him. Among the kinds of background knowledge, the one with the greatest moral content is obviously religious knowledge. Since this class of knowledge will be treated separately, we need only mention it here. Other knowledges and their influence on assents need not be taken separately. For our present purpose it is sufficient merely to note that former knowledge is one factor influencing the assents of the student.

Besides his knowledge, the student before entering the college classroom has developed moral habits and social manners. The presence of such habits has something to do with his learning. Aristotle points out that only students who have been brought up in good habits can listen intelligently to lectures on ethics.[2] The reason he gives is that a line of reasoning must have a starting point in the knowledge of the learner. The student must know that some acts are good and noble before he can come to the principle that will explain why these acts are good and noble. What would justify a moral principle unless it were found in facts; that is, in acts known to be good? The student raised to bad habits will have no starting point for a rational ethics, though he will have starting points, such as pleasure or willfulness or greed, for rationalizing his bad actions. A better place to see clearly the effect of bad choices on understanding is in the man of advanced viciousness. The truly unjust man gets to the stage where other men's just acts appear to him as acts arising from stupidity or spinelessness. He simply cannot understand how any man using his mind would pass up an opportunity to take money from naive (honest) fools. His bad will is an active factor that has warped his mind to see only those aspects or facts that can be at peace with his bad will. Besides modifying assent, bad habits can also stop the act of learning. A student who has committed himself to sensible pleasure will either not begin to study because it is unpleasant or not continue because he finds the learning process difficult.

The third factor proper and personal to the learner is the state of his sense appetites. When emotions hold sway, they influence mental assents. Some emotions—such as hate, aversion, sadness, despair, fear, anger—make all reasoning processes so difficult as to be either impossible or unreliable. Some emotions—love, desire, delight—can make reasoning acts easier and more pleasant, provided, of course, that the object of these emotions is something that is related to knowledge. When their object is something foreign to learning, they, too, make reasoning difficult and unreliable. The student whose emotions reinforce his life of learning is the avid student, who is the dream of every teacher.

Finally, for purposes of completeness, something should be said about the sense faculties of the learner. These play an important role in the learning of speculative knowledge.[3] Without the sense powers the mind would have nothing to think about, since it is through our senses that we encounter things. Through sensation we get our beginning data. When sense data are properly prepared and held steady for continuous inspection, the mind can do its work accurately. Poorly prepared sense images make intellectual knowledge incomplete or erroneous; just as the failure to hold them steady for continued consideration makes intellectual knowledge superficial. A student who has no interest in mathematics finds in mathematical problems no images he is willing to examine very long at a time. His knowledge of mathematics will be erroneous or superficial because of his natural disposition, which must be modified before he can learn mathematics at all well. However natural disposition can be modified, its presence and influence are active determinants of sensation and, as such, are operative in the act of learning speculative knowledge. So much for the active conditions of learning that arise from the student himself.

We turn now to the second class of existential conditions influencing student minds; namely, those arising from the teacher. Students make their taught assents under the instrumental activity of the teacher. The teacher in turn teaches what he knows, and what he knows includes both the subject matter and the way he understands it. A teacher who understands his subject in one way will teach students to understand the subject in the same way. Thus a teacher who is only a specialist in one limited field can only impart knowledge of the subject matter as a limited specialty because that is the only way he knows it. Again, from a large body of data some facts must be selected for presentation in class. Among the selected data some must be emphasized. The selection of, and emphasis put on, data are, within certain bounds, up to the teacher. The principle of selection and emphasis will again be what he knows, including of course the way he knows it. Finally, the very intellectual personality of the teacher is present in his teaching. By intellectual personality is meant the moral characteristics of his own knowing acts, such as intellectual honesty, persevering care for accuracy, justice to other knowers—in a word, either the teacher's love of the truth or its opposite, his love of himself as knowing. A word now about each of these three ways in which the teacher sets up the conditions influencing the learner's acts of reasoning.

First, the condition of knowing set up by the way the teacher presents his subject matter. A teacher who has a competent grasp of moral and religious truths will not leave unmentioned these larger truths when the proper occasion presents itself. Thus an economic question that has social and moral aspects needs to be related to these other aspects of the question. And it needs this relating in the very name of economics. Economics is precisely the partial aspect of what in reality is a whole. The life of man has its economic aspects, which truly are partial aspects of the life of man. Not to know this is not to know something very important about economics. The teacher who indicates the moral or social suppositions and consequences of an economic solution is precisely keeping both himself and his students in the field of economics. He gets both himself and his students out of economics when he thinks that moral issues are primarily economic or that solving an economic problem automatically solves the moral problems. It may pay to be honest, but honesty is a virtue even when it does not pay. The economist, as economist, has no principles for solving moral problems and therefore should not attempt the impossible, just as the moralist qua moralist has no principles for solving economic problems; and therefore he, too, should not attempt the impossible. But solving problems is not the same as indicating their relevance. The moralist teacher who simply ignores the economic aspect of a problem of commutative justice is not a teacher worth listening to. By the

same token, an economist who ignores every moral implication of his economic conclusions is not much of a teacher
of economics.[4]

Now, let us take a student learning his economics from
a teacher who points out, when the need arises, the moral
implications of an economic conclusion. This student will
have learned economics in an actual setting that modifies
his understanding of economics. Economics will stand in
his mind as a knowledge which is properly limited to one
aspect of a larger whole—man's manipulation and exchange of material reality. Let us make the opposite supposition of a student who is taught economics with no
relation to any other knowledge. Economics can easily
stand in his mind as a body of knowledge which, single-
handed, deals adequately with man's business life. No one
need convince him of this. It is easy for him to take it for
granted. Economics explains man's business life. Other
aspects besides the economic are not worth mentioning,
seeing that his teacher sees no need to mention them. A
student, so taught, could easily suppose that economics is
the whole story about man's business life. That is the way
he learned his economics because that is the way it was
taught him.[5] And notice that our quarrel is not with his
economic conclusions. These, by supposition, are faultless
as conclusions from principle and data about economic
objects. Our quarrel is with the teacher's mind in which
these conclusions actually exist. The room is too bare. A
table without chairs is still a good table. But if one knows
nothing of chairs, he might be found at last sitting on the
table, primarily because there are no chairs around.

The second active condition modifying learned knowledge arises from the teacher's free decision concerning

103

how best to present this matter. Not that he can teach anything other than the subject matter—not and be a teacher of this subject. The intelligibility, and teachability, of a subject consists precisely in explaining the relevant data. Such he must explain or not be a teacher. Yet there is a spot where he must freely make decisions. For example, the amount of emphasis to be given to this or that phase or part of the material to be taught, what examples he will use, what references he will make to supplementary or complementary data or subjects. The presumption is, of course, that such free decisions by the teacher grow out of his knowledge. When they grow out of his passions, such freedom is nothing more than license. When these free decisions grow out of his knowledge of both the subject and the students to be taught, his freedom is that proper to the living teacher. For it is these free decisions of how subjects are to be presented that constitute the very art of the teacher, as we said above.

Consider the matter of emphasis. Here a relatively minor variation in emphasis can flavor the student's understanding of the data. One who wishes to test this proposition can examine the emphasis that V. L. Parrington, in his well-known *Main Currents in American Thought*, puts on the personal idiosyncracies of the seventeenth-century American religious thinkers. No doubt many of these thinkers did not have particularly attractive personalities. Yet neither their nor any man's thought should be judged by the charm or rigidity of the person thinking. But a student who reads Parrington's account can hardly keep from thinking these men were second-rate thinkers. Not that Parrington says this in so many words. What encourages the reader to make that conclusion is the realization that they were clearly odd characters. And this realization arises solely from the emphasis Parrington chose to put on the personalities of these religious thinkers.

A similar effect can be produced by the examples chosen for purposes of explanation, when the examples are taken from common experience or from other fields of specialized knowledge. In such cases of teaching, the intellectual content of the example is not being taught. The very reason for using examples of this kind is to find in more familiar material a case of what the student must see in the less familiar material being taught. Thus the very effectiveness of the example depends on its content being taken for granted. Recall the example used in the last paragraph concerning early American religious thinkers. It serves the purpose of explanation only on the supposition that the reader agrees with this, that a man's thought is not wrong because his personality is unpleasant. Accept this proposition as true and the example used exemplifies; reject the proposition as false and the example I used exemplifies nothing to you. Thus examples of this sort require agreement as the condition of their serving as examples. They can also carry implications. Castell's *College Logic*, for example, builds up an implication concerning the prohibition amendment. In dealing with fallacies, he has a number of examples taken from the writings of those who defended the Eighteenth Amendment. Every example he gives is an excellent teaching example of a fallacy. Yet the very number of them impels a student towards the conclusion that the prohibitionist position was fundamentally unreasonable. Castell was not proposing to make this point; he proposed to explain the logic of fallacies. Still, his choice of examples did a bit more than merely explain fallacies by examples; it also quietly but effectively built up a position against prohibition.

Beyond emphasis and examples there is the matter of asides and parenthetical comments of the teacher. Not the perverse sort, which do not pertain to the subject matter and arise therefore from the teacher's love of his own opinions. These hardly need be noticed further than to score them as acts of intellectual injustice perpetrated on a captive audience. But there are pertinent asides and comments that all teachers make. For example, the Christian teacher discussing segregation in a sociology class could hardly be expected not to indicate his opinion of the immorality of segregation. And even if he did, he could not appeal to the nature of teaching to justify his refusal to state at least his moral judgment of segregation. He could, of course, appeal to the nature of sociology and stand on his right and duty as a sociologist to teach sociological, rather than moral, conclusions. So far, so good. But the teaching sociologist in this case is also a man. The teacher's job as both sociologist and man is to do his best to help his students understand, in this case, segregation. This best of his may well include indicating briefly what he considers important for any educated man to know about segregation and therefore important for the students before him. Obviously, he is bound by his duty as teacher to indicate that the moral judgment he makes is not a sociological conclusion but a moral judgment, for that is what it is. But to demand that teachers of sociology refrain from all statements that are not formally sociological is to forget that the teacher is also a man. Even where the teacher's parenthetical remarks are not valid—say, those of the psychologist who thinks that all religion is superstitious and remarks to that effect when teaching the psychology of scruples—he should be criticized not so much for making nonpsychological remarks as for making unfounded nonpsychological remarks. His weakness is not that he makes parenthetical remarks; his weakness is that he knows too little to be a teacher of men. And the proper solution to this problem is for the student, or school, to find a teacher of psychology who also knows something about religion.

While considering the teacher's remarks that go outside his formal subject matter, some reference must be made to the role of the teacher's faith, even though we shall consider this more fully later. For there are times when a teacher may, while teaching other subject matter, make direct reference to a truth of faith. If a teacher's mind has developed under the love of God and the illumination of his faith, all his root values and ultimate suppositions will be grounded in, or at least not be incompatible with, his faith. On occasion a student may get a glimpse of these fundamentals behind what he is being taught and inquire about the connections of such truths. He has a right to be answered; and consequently the teacher has the duty to answer such questions, if he can. On occasion, too, the teacher's very presentation of subject matter makes him acutely aware of the connections of his present thought with his faith. To be honest with his students he may well have to interrupt briefly his impersonal presentation of the matter and show how personally and for himself the line of his present thought is anchored in his faith.[6] This in no way destroys the objectivity of his teaching. He is teaching what he knows in the way he knows it at the moment. No more can be asked of any teacher, and no less. Not only Christian but atheistic teachers may do something similar when it comes to indicating fundamental suppositions. The answer to this problem is not to emasculate the teacher by refusing him the right to do the best he can as a teacher, even if it is not very good. The answer seems rather to have Christian colleges and universities.

Whatever one thinks the proper solution to such situations may be, no one will deny that the teacher's parenthetical remarks are operative on the knowledge coming to the student. Unless the student violently disagrees with such asides, he will hardly notice them. And when they go unnoticed, they are especially effective in modifying the student's assent. Examples used and emphasis placed operate in the same fashion. For the knowledge comes to him clothed in these examples, ordered under this emphasis and accompanied by these parenthetical remarks. His assents quite naturally fit into the same actual framework as those under which the knowledge comes to him. After all, the teacher is supposed to know his subject and how to explain it. The student has enough to do to get the principles and conclusions of what he is being taught. He can hardly be expected to criticize all the teacher's free decisions regarding examples, emphasis, parenthetical remarks. Moreover, if the student were up to checking each of these factors of teaching, he would hardly need a teacher.

Among the factors operative on the student making assents the teacher himself is extremely influential. He is intimately tied in with the student's activity of forming conclusions from data and principles. When a student knows, it is, of course, his own act, not the teacher's. Yet until he does know, his mind is related to what he knows as an active power to its activity. Now, an active power needs only to be present to what will complete it and then it goes into activity. Think of the human eye faced with the colored object. To be an eye is to respond in activity to the present object actually colored. With proper qualifications, the human mind is like the eye in that it, too, will flower in activity when faced with the reasoning process in act. Here is where the teacher enters. It is his task to go through—that is, to make actual and present to the student—the reasoning process from principles and data to conclusion. If he succeeds in making his own reasoning process present in act to the student's mind—and this is the art of teaching—then the active mental power of the student will answer this present act. Thus the teacher's thought stands as the living sign of reasoning in this subject matter. The student's taught knowledge stands as what, though before unformed, is now formed to a similar state of actual thought, thanks to the living model before him. Notice that the tie-in between the teacher's and the student's knowledge is on two levels: (*a*) there is similarity, so that one is like the other; (*b*) the student's knowledge is actual because the teacher's knowledge is actual. On both levels, therefore, the teacher is most intimately involved in the assents made by the student.

This involvement, centered in the reasoning process, is essential to all complete teaching. Important therefore as it is, it is not the only involvement of the teacher in the student's learning, nor is it the first in time. For the student's mind is not present with a pure thought process but with a teacher thinking. The living model before him is a man going about the job of thinking. Through the man he gets at the man's thought. If the man is a sincere, careful, precise, humble thinker, his very thought will live under these qualities. If he is intellectually vain or lazy or shallow or proud, his thought will be burdened with such a fault. And whatever his thought is blessed or burdened with, so also is his teaching.

The vain man, for instance, puts excessive store by his own knowledge and intellectual acumen. He tends to consider his knowledge as something new and unheard of before him, because original ideas are especially prized by men. For the same reason, the very latest ideas have a particular fascination for him, as in some way justifying his own emphasis on the novel. When teaching, such a thinker does not spend much time in class on what the great thinkers of the past have said but prefers to dismiss their conclusions with flippant observations that prove, not his grasp of the problem, but only his cleverness. Of course, he wants to be right, or else he would hardly be called a thinker and certainly should not be a teacher; but he also wants to be clever. Faced with a choice between the two, he prefers to be a bit less true in order to be a bit more clever. This is the way he thinks outside of class; this consequently is the way he thinks in class—though it could as well be the other way around. At any rate, the student, following such a teacher, might easily slip into the same way of thinking. Cleverness would become one of the recognizable marks of truth. And a cleverly stated opinion would gain the student's assent more because it was flashy than because it was founded in facts. No doubt, the student is somewhat at fault for going along with the teacher's vanity. But if the teacher is to be the student's living model of how to think in this subject matter, why should not the student try to carry on his thinking just as his teacher does?

Imitation, of course, supposes respect for the one being imitated. And since teaching deals with knowledge, the respect of the student for the teacher must first touch the teacher as one who knows what he is talking about. Even students not thrilled by the life of learning do not miss the obvious point that teaching requires knowledge in the teacher. Personal charm is no substitute for it. Where there is very little knowledge in act there is very little for the student's mind to rise to. Consequently there is no experience of learning that would ground respect for the teacher as knower, no matter how likable he might be. Nor is there any reason why the student would want to think as his teacher does.

Not all students, however, are up to estimating correctly the teacher's true competence in knowledge. Young college students easily confuse mental agility with profundity and rhetorical facility with brilliance. They can therefore be taken in at the point where they could apply a norm. The only spot at which a student, who supposedly does not know what he is to learn, can judge the competence of the teacher's knowledge is his own experience of learning from this teacher. He respects a teacher's knowledge because he learned from him. Mental agility and rhetorical facility can produce in the inexperienced student an impression of learning that will perhaps satisfy until the student meets real knowledge in his own experience. But once he has followed a real knower at work and knows what good knowing is by having done it, he will condemn shallow substitutes for knowing and the shallow teachers who took him in. By the same token, the teacher who is sincere and careful and accurate gains enormously in the respect of knowing students.

This respect for the teacher, important as it is in the personal relation of student and teacher, has an important role also in the very act of knowing, where it increases the intellectual receptivity of the student. For the student is in a very special situation as a learner. To put oneself under a teacher is a commitment with moral consequences. The student, coming to the teacher for the first time, must suppose that the teacher knows. Yet he cannot trade on this supposition by following the teacher blindly, not if he ever hopes to know for himself. He must, in the beginning, be testing the prudence of his decision to commit himself to this teacher. The careful, precise, humble teacher solves this prudential problem of the student by the patent virtues of his life of thought. Secure in his first commitment, the student can release his whole energy for the task of knowing, with the aid of this teacher, what is true or what is not, or along which lines he can hope to discover the truth. He therefore becomes more receptive because his mind is freer to concentrate on the task of understanding.[7] And the opposite, of course, is equally true. The student faced with the thought of a vain or self-centered teacher finds himself constantly forced to put brakes on his spontaneity. How much has vanity or selfishness colored this opinion or warped this line of reasoning? Is some striking statement of the teacher a profound insight worth struggling for, or is it the child of a vain desire to astound, worth no more than a moment's entertainment in a long class period? The mere suspicion that the second alternative is true blocks the student's intellectual receptivity. Knock off, and let the clown try for laughs. Not only is no student assent made; not even enough attention is given to find out if there was anything said worth close consideration. And what blocked all intellectual activity and dried up all curiosity is not the difficulty of the problem or the student's lassitude; it is the faults of the teacher. The student sitting before a teacher whom he is not willing to imitate is a student with his mental blinds drawn.

Granted respect for the teacher, the natural desire to imitate goes beyond the purely intellectual sphere. The student can see more than the teacher's intellectual competence because more is actually present before him. That more is the man. Not all of man's moral qualities appear in his life of teaching. Some do, especially the virtues of friendliness and justice. The teacher who is considerate, gracious, tactful, and friendly commands a respect as a man that flows back on to what he teaches by creating the atmosphere of good will and moral security. The suspicious or rude or inconsiderate teacher will have the opposite influence on the student, for the man is getting in the way of his teaching. As for justice, this virtue holds a special place in teaching, just as it does in all human relations. It shows up in the way the teacher faces those who disagree with him. More noticeable to the student, it shows up in the teacher's decisions where he has authority—in assigning grades, in demands on the time of the student, and so on. When the student can respect both the teacher as man and the teacher as knower, he will find it normal to try to become himself a man as knower with similar human characteristics.

We began our analysis of the teacher's influence on student assent by distinguishing the teacher as thinker from the teacher as man. We arrived at the realization that in the concrete the student sees before him only one thing, the living teacher carrying on his intellectual life before him. He sees a man thinking his thoughts, with fundamental suppositions grounded in faith, relating his thoughts to other fields, using this emphasis, these examples, making these parenthetical remarks—all this activity informed by the moral virtues of friendliness and justice. Here before the student is the excellence of knowing in all its concrete richness. Why should he not model his knowing on this admirable example before him? That he does would not surprise the metaphysician who would report the facts thus—active power tends to answer present operative act. The same fact would be reported by the psychologist in the following way. The student, aware that he must become what he hopes to be, sees before him what he would like to become, a human person knowing this subject matter. Once a student finds a teacher who commands his full respect, the limits to which the student will imitate the teacher are not easily set—extending at times to such inconsequential mannerism as tone of voice, distinctive inflections and gestures, even to cut of clothes and hair.

We turn now to the third class of circumstances that influence the assent of the learner; namely, those arising from his faith. Two remarks are in place here. The first is that these circumstances as we shall describe them will be operative only in a Catholic college. The second remark is that our neat parceling of the morally significant conditions of assent into three groups should not lead one to think that the faith is just one of three influences, all of which are on an equal footing. Nothing could be further from the truth. The faith in a Catholic college is the active condition of assents, permeating and modifying not only the assents of the learner but the other active influences as well; that is, the state of emotions and the attitudes of the teacher. The only justification for putting the influences of the faith in a group of their own is to be clearer about the way the faith influences student assents.

There is no question about the faith influencing assents by coming in between data-problem-principle-conclusion of a line of reasoning. If it did that, it would take the very reasonableness out of such natural learning. We have insisted on this point above and here repeat it for further emphasis. Nothing whatever, not even another kind of fact, can break into the line from fact to conclusion without violating the whole process. But merely because the faith does not enter the line of reasoning does not mean that it has nothing to do with such assents. The faith exists in the minds of the student and teacher; through its presence in their minds it affects the assents of both. That the faith can do this is best seen by seeing how it does it.

The faith itself consists in assents to the word of God. God has revealed truths about Himself, about man, about the world, about man's relation to the world, to other men, and to God. The faith, as a Catholic understands it, is therefore a series of truths to which the mind assents on the authority of God.[8] Once such assents are made, there are consequences for action. Thus if God has instituted a Church with the authortity to teach and interpret His revelation—and this is Catholic faith—it follows that the Church must be listened to in matters of faith and morals. In matters of knowledge the Church acts by teaching and defining doctrines. In matters of action the Church acts by setting up disciplinary regulations. The Catholic is thus obligated to assenting to certain doctrines as truths revealed by God and to acting according to disciplinary regulations. Catholic students are likewise bound to both doctrine and discipline. And both of these come into the life of learning.

For our present purposes we shall not consider the assents of faith as acts of knowledge in their own field (which they are) but rather as conditions that affect assents in other fields. The faith as well as other morally related kinds of knowledge has much to do with the morality of students. In Chapter 7 we shall have occasion to consider the part such knowledge plays in moral choices. At present we are trying to see how the faith modifies the assents made by reason working naturally in any of the arts and sciences taught in colleges. Obviously, the faith considered here is a knowledge that can stand eye-level with the arts and sciences taught in college; that is, faith at the scientific level of theology. What a grammar-school knowledge of faith could do for college-acquired knowledge is hard to imagine; it might, indeed, get in the way. At any rate, there would be no point to our consideration unless we supposed that the knowledge of faith be developed to a stage comparable with that of the other knowledges taught in college.

We distinguished the components of the faith as doctrines and consequent disciplinary regulations. Since these will modify other assents differently, we shall consider them separately, as is proper. And the right ordering would be to take doctrinal influence first as being more important. There is only one disciplinary regulation—that of the Index of Prohibited Books—that affects student assents in the arts and sciences, and it does so infrequently. However, in the minds of most people, especially of non-Catholics, this regulation is seen as the major way in which the faith affects—here *affects* means "blocks"—learning. It is untrue, as any Catholic scholar knows from experience. But this fact does nothing to change the minds of those who have not experienced the fact. Hence arises a rhetorical problem. Until the Index has been treated in its negative aspect, readers may feel that they are being put off. They might not be in the mood to give serious attention to the more important role of the faith in modifying student assents. For rhetorical reasons, then, we shall honor the readers' preference by taking the Index first, with the understanding that its true importance will be shown when our analysis arrives at the point where consideration of the Index, as both negative and positive, properly belongs.

The disciplinary regulation that establishes the Index of Prohibited Books is Canon 1399 of the Code of Canon Law. This canon lists some ten categories of books,[9] of which the following might conceivably touch college students: books defending heresy and schism or attacking the foundations of religion; books whose principal purpose is to attack religion and good morals; books attacking or ridiculing any dogma of the Catholic Church; books that are professedly lascivious; translations of the Holy Scripture that are not approved by the Church. On the basis of the norms of Canon 1399, the Church publishes a list of the books that are proscribed by name.[10]

How does this disciplinary regulation affect a college student's assent? Strictly speaking, it does not modify assents, for its effect is prior to the act of assenting. What it does is exclude certain matter from the student's consideration. He may not examine these books in order to judge their worth. Take the case of lascivious books. A college student may not read such books. His intellectual posture before them is as follows: he knows or can know, from spontaneous reasoning as well as from his faith, that lascivious books, if there are any, are not to be examined by him because of their probable effect on his moral and religious life. That this or that book is lascivious he knows only from the word of another, not because he himself examined the book. Thus he can make the prudential decision that he should not read this lascivious book. But the college student may not—cannot and still follow his faith—examine what he knows from competent persons are lascivious books in order to decide for himself that they are lascivious.

Lascivious books might seem to be a privileged case, but what is true of them is true of all the kinds of books excluded. The same principle holds for all of them; namely, such books are considered harmful to the moral and religious life of unformed students. When students become competent and have need to read prohibited books, they may easily get permission to read them. Until they become competent, it seems the part of prudence to protect them against what they cannot cope with. Some defenders of intellectual freedom get so wrapped up in their worthy task that they fail to see the reasonableness of the prudential principle of protecting those who cannot protect themselves. The reasonableness of this principle is easily recognized in any neutral situation where the charge of censorship is not likely. The American Library Association, for instance, refers to the librarian's "important function of fitting books to the personal needs of individual readers" so as to "develop desirable reading habits and tastes in boys and girls."[11] It seems sensible to suppose that one could not develop desirable habits and tastes by reading books that would encourage him to be morally worse off than he was before he was given such books. Even John Milton, the most eloquent defender of freedom of publication, bears witness to the reasonableness of excluding some books from publication. Though most books should not be denied publication, he would not tolerate "popery and open superstition—that also which is impious or evil absolutely either against faith or manners . . ."[12] In the name of reason the Church agrees with Milton that clearly harmful books are not to be published, and with the American Library Association that the young develop reading tastes that are not harmful.[13]

The reasonableness of the disciplinary regulations of the faith, however, is not our main interest at present. Here we are considering how the regulations touch the reasoned assents of a college student. Their effect is therefore not to modify assents but to exclude them by excluding the consideration of certain matter. So considered, disciplinary regulations are negative in that they exclude the possibility of assents. In this way disciplinary regulations differ from the doctrines of faith. These latter never block assents; they always modify and improve assents being given to data fully considered and examined. We turn now to see what this modifying action of faith is.

We shall consider four major ways in which the faith modifies assents made in other fields. First, the faith on occasion purifies and improves too hasty conclusions in the arts and sciences. Second, the faith aids reason so that true assents can be made with greater ease. Third, the faith reinforces the assents of reason in the vital area of morally related knowledge. Fourth, the faith humanizes the assents made in the arts and sciences. Each of these modifying actions will be considered separately, beginning with the first.

The role of faith as purifier of conclusions in the arts and sciences does not mean that the faith stands and cracks a whip over other knowledges, keeping them in line. If such were true, there would be no arts and sciences. Recall that these knowledges have their own data, principles, and conclusions; they need no other knowledge to justify them or tell them what to say, nor can any outside knowledge do that. But it remains true that thinkers, any thinker, can make hasty conclusions, so that this or that conclusion may have only the presumption and not the substance of reasonableness. When this happens, any outside knowledge, and not only the faith, may put one in a position to point out the lack of reasonableness.[14] The faith is, however, in an especially advantageous position to do this work for the sciences because it is not a man-made knowledge but a God-given one. How it does this is best seen in specific cases.

Consider the biological theory of evolution. Biologists generally consider it proved that man as a living species evolved from a lower species of living being. The biologist's direct concern here is man's organic life, his peculiar organs and their structures and activities. Since the evidence points to their development from a lower form of life, biologists generally conclude that man evolved. Now, one may hold that the organic evidence leads him to conclude that man has evolved organically from lower organisms. This conclusion is reasonable or not depending on the amount and weight of the evidence the natural sciences discover. But even granting that the evidence is overwhelming for the organic evolution of man, that same

evidence will not of itself account for the nonorganic factor in man, his reflective thought. Reflective thought in
man does require a relatively large and involuted brain.
That such a brain evolved from less developed brains or
less developed living cells or even from nonliving matter
is not impossible.[15] What seems impossible is that a brain
should be anything more than a condition for reflective
thought. The brain is material; reflective thought, whatever it is, cannot be material. If man is a being with reflective thought, he is more than just an organism or body;
he is also partly spiritual. Consequently, the evidence that
permits one to say man's body evolved will not be enough
to justify saying that man, a unit of body and spiritual
soul, evolved. Nor would a mind possessed of the faith be
able to overlook this spirituality of man's soul. As a result
it could not possibly examine the biological data and fall
into the mistake of saying that man evolved merely because his body did.

A scientist could rejoin that contemporary biology
knows little of the human soul and nothing of its spirituality; therefore he, as a biologist, need not take this fact
as data to ground his biological conclusions. In this he is
dead right. To introduce a spiritual soul into biology
would ruin biology, which would be bad enough; what is
worse, it would undermine any adequate understanding
of the spirituality of the soul. But it remains true that no
thinker should make statements about things of which he
is admittedly ignorant. And to say that man evolved is to
say something about the spiritual soul of man and not
merely something about his body. Those who do not wish
to talk about the spiritual will have to forego talking about
man and clearly indicate their self-imposed limitation.

Nothing helps one to see this limitation better than the truths of faith.

Our second example showing how the faith purifies too hasty conclusions is not limited to one art or science but introduces a possible by-product of any of them; namely, intellectual imperialism. When treating of reflectively elaborated knowledge (in Chapter 4) we said this kind of knowledge could protect one from intellectual imperialism, which substitutes a part for the whole. It reminds the specialists in the arts and sciences that they have only the knowledge of men and that there is another kind of knowledge, the revelation of God, which is not like their knowledge. Faith is knowledge and not like the human arts and sciences. Consequently, all the arts and sciences are not the whole of knowledge. And if all of them are not the whole of knowledge, clearly one of them is not. A student with the faith, for instance, could hardly agree with John Dewey that all good thought is like the thinking done in the physical sciences.[16] He would see immediately that Dewey is magnifying a part into the whole, that he is making a tree into a forest—a forest that hides the rest of the countryside from his view.

Moreover, the student with a good understanding of his faith could also see what is wrong with John Dewey's position. Before all the facts are in, Dewey is setting up by human decree what things can be known validly. The ground for his desire is not what is but his admiration for one way of knowing. The valid object of knowledge is no longer what is but what is susceptible of being known by his method. These facts, the kind his method will handle, and only these can be admitted as data; all others must be thrown down the disposal. No intellectual posture could make less sense than this self-blinding does to one with faith. Man's knowledge is little enough without his making his own earplugs to keep him from hearing what God has revealed about Himself, such as the mysteries of the Trinity and the Incarnation. Once a mind has been nourished on mysteries, asking it to limit all truth to what is acquired by some man-made method of knowing is to ask it to stultify itself. It knows some truths, the most important for human life, not acquired or acquirable by the scientific method or by any other man-made technique.

Again, the student with faith could see the error of disposing of all data not suitable to one method of knowing. In the face of data, man can understand it or not. He cannot unmake it because he did not make it. God did. Man can choose what sort of data he wishes to think about, but he cannot decree data out of existence. That a philosopher handles only philosophical facts makes sense. That a philosopher takes a further step and decrees that all facts are philosophical or that what is not philosophical is not a fact—this makes no sense. And what is true of philosophers and philosophy is true of all human ways of knowing. Data are God-given. To explain some part of the data gives no man the right to say anything about the part he does not explain.

Thus the faith in the student's mind helps him to purify the too hasty conclusion that constitutes intellectual imperialism. He can agree that the scientific method is a good method of knowing some kinds of facts; he cannot agree that it is the only valid method of knowing. The presence in his mind of revealed mysteries, besides the realization that God created the world that is our data, helps him to see what is wrong with intellectual imperialism.[17]

The second way in which the faith influences student assents is by making the student's work easier. Sometimes the faith offers specific insights that reason can exploit to achieve clearer and firmer assents than reason, left to itself, ever achieved. At all times the faith, by presenting a vision of the world that is beyond but not contrary to reason, gives reason a head start in its own work of understanding the world. Both of these influences, the specific and general, need to be spelled out. We shall consider them separately in spite of their obvious connection.

One example of an insight supplied by faith concerns the nature of the dignity of man. Spontaneous knowledge says that man is a cut above all the other beings on the earth. But it does not say why this is so. Reflection is needed to give the reason for man's superiority. Human reflection has supplied many reasons: that man is free, that he has reason, that he is an artist, that he is a maker of tools, that he can use animals to serve his needs, that he is a higher form in the process of evolution, that he can harness and wield greater power. Each of these reasons has some validity, but they do not hang together well enough. If power is the basis of man's superiority over animals, there is not much left for freedom or reason to do. Again, if reason or freedom is the basis, man's evolutionary status is of no critical importance. And using animals to meet his needs has little relation to his being toolmaker or artist. The problem here is not that only one of the reasons given is true and that we lack the power to distinguish the true reason from the false ones. All the reasons given are true enough, as common experience testifies. What they lack is some intelligible unity among themselves. The faith supplies that unity.

Man is superior to animals, the faith tells us, because he is the image and likeness of God. This constitutes man's dignity, that he is the image of God. He is free, has reason, is an artist and a toolmaker, can use animals (which are not like God) for his own ends, can wield power, and is a higher form of life precisely because he is like God. His destiny is to be with God. Hence the many powers he possesses. Any one of them will show his superiority over animals. But behind them all, giving unity to man's nature and to our understanding of that nature, is the central reason that man is the image of God.

With this insight from faith, reason understands more easily what man is and in what his dignity consists. He is made for God, not for other men or for the state. Neither man nor the state has the right to interfere with his seeking God. To interfere with knowledge is to block man's finding God. Hence the dignity of man's intellect. To interfere with choices is to block man's love of God. Hence the dignity of man's freedom. No one has the right to violate either a man's mind or his will because man is made for the knowledge and love of God.

The strength of this insight can best be shown negatively, by showing what happens to the understanding of the dignity of man when this insight does not aid reason. Pagan civilization of the past could show us some faulty understandings of man.[18] But we can find evidence much closer to us in time and culture. The American Declaration of Independence states: "We hold these truths to be self-evident, that all men are created equal, that they are endowed by their Creator with certain unalienable Rights, that among these are Life, Liberty and the pursuit of Happiness." These words, whether they are Jefferson's personal views or not, express a view of man that came from revelation. I say "came from," though they fall considerably short of the picture of man that Christian revelation gives. The words "created" and "endowed by their Creator," as used in the Declaration, might mislead one until he backs off a bit and looks at what is being said. The ground is reason—these truths are "self-evident"— and not the word of God. And the whole issue of equality among men is reduced to something natively proper to the individual—these "unalienable Rights." The essential doctrine of the Declaration can be kept entire even if we strike out the words "created" and "endowed by their Creator." What the document would say is that reason guarantees that men are equal because born with unalienable rights among which . . . and so on. That is what it says as it stands.

Thirteen years later, in August of 1789, the French National Assembly, on the eve of the French Revolution, adopted the Declaration of the Rights of Man. Here, too, God appears but now in the more ambiguous role of the Supreme Being; not even the word "creator" is kept. What justifies the "natural, inalienable and sacred Rights of Man" is their status as "simple and indisputable principles."[19] Men now find the source of their dignity not in their being images of God and destined to know and love Him. God must be pushed out of the picture so that man can be exalted. Thereby they decree, in the name of reason, what reason by itself has never made stick.

The intellectual punishment for giving the wrong answer is not merely that the right one gets lost but that all get lost, even the wrong one. To say that it is self-evident that all men are created equal is to invite reason to justify the equality of men. What reason discovers is precisely the opposite, that men are not equal, either in physical or mental or moral qualities. What, then, happens to the rights of man? If these are to be the same for all, some source other than native excellence (which is not equal) must be found. The handiest source is the state, which endows all with equal rights before the law. The only problem with this solution is that it destroys the possibility of inalienable rights. What the state can give it can take away. In principle, then, man has no dignity as the source of inalienable rights; and in principle the state is not constituted merely to protect inalienable rights, since it bestows them. In man's place a creature of man, the state, acquires the dignity proper to the source of human rights. It will call the tune, and he must dance to it or get off the floor.

We have attended the demise of a good idea not in order to act as prophet but to see what happens to reason when it loses an insight from faith. Had reason kept before it the real grounds for man's dignity—the image of God and divine destiny—it would have had firm ground on which to build its own defense of man's dignity. Without this insight, reason can only move from one sandbar to the other, hoping always to find another when its present footing washes away. It may succeed, but it does so only with infinite embarrassment to reason itself. Here the faith could help reason make firmer and more lasting assents and consequently be more reasonable.

Besides specific insights, the faith helps reason by supplying a general vision of the world and reason's understanding of the world. This vision is, of course, beyond what reason can supply; but it is only beyond, not against.

The difference is profound. Were faith against reason, each supplying opposed and incompatible visions, the student, if he continued to think, would have to choose one and reject the other. But he could do this on no reasonable grounds. The faith would stand as certainly true, with the truth of God to back it. Reason, too, would stand as certainly true, with the self-evident principles of reason as assurance. Not being able to deny either he could affirm neither. No assents would be possible.

Moreover, it is not sufficient merely that faith should not be against reason. It must also be beyond, if it is to be of any help to reason. Suppose the faith said the same thing reason could say. What need would there be of reason? It could profitably be neglected as a poor way of doing what was already done better. But if the faith gives a vision beyond that of reason, there are two visions; and there is the possibility that faith and reason can help each other in their own proper work.

We are interested here in showing how the faith actually helps reason understand the world. The vision of the world given by faith can be stated very briefly in this way. God created the world freely. He created man to His image, with intellect to know Him and will to love Him and thereby gain participation in the life of God. Man refused this offer and then the Father sent His Son to redeem man and make possible man's return, through the presence of the Holy Spirit, to his true destiny of participating in the life of God. Reason could never construct such a vision of reality shot through as it is with mysteries. Yet no vision ever presented by reason is anywhere near as reasonable. No philosopher from Aristotle to Whitehead has said anything half so sensible. No artist from

Homer to Hemingway, from Praxiteles to Picasso, has even come close. As for the natural scientists, Newton's picture of the world looked so much like a heartless cosmic machine that even he got worried and tried, in the second edition of his *Principia Mathematica,* to bootleg God into his celestial mechanics, to the advantage of neither. And contemporary physicists are not even agreed on what picture they should present.

Compared to the many world-pictures given by reason, that of the faith has two qualities that aid reason in its work. The first is that it can serve reason at any stage of its development. The child just beginning to think finds himself in an intelligible world, with a Father in heaven as well as a father on earth. The college student, just beginning to understand the ideal of the sciences, finds that his faith, raised to the level of theology, can answer scientifically what the human sciences must leave unsaid. And the scholar, working at the frontiers of knowledge, can find in the mysteries of revelation a source of light for seeing what are not mysteries.

The second quality of the faith-given vision of the world is its stability. It does not change with each new discovery of man, as the sciences must do. They live and grow on the discoveries of men and therefore change regularly. We are inclined to think of the natural sciences as the most reliable and steady knowledge man can attain. Yet the history of physics shows that its theories are becoming progressively shorter in their life-span. "The universes of sciences now succeed one another with a curiously accelerated speed. Like the patriarchs of the Old Testament, they seem to obey a law of diminishing longevity. The system of Ptolemy died fourteen centuries ago, which was a ripe old age; that of Copernicus, which replaced it, lasted almost three centuries; that of Einstein lasted twenty-two years . . ."[20] Scientific theory must change to account for newly discovered facts. But the faith is not a discovered knowledge; it is a given knowledge, given by Christ once and for all. Nor is the faith subject to the popular pressure of fads as the arts are. They must be responsive to the demands of contemporary man because their role is to serve man, who is always contemporary. The faith does not serve man by changing to fit his views. Rather, man must answer to the demands of faith. The faith, therefore, stands above discoveries and temporary pressures. Hence its power to aid reason. For its vision of the world is a steady light man can rely on, a sure point to start from and return to when reason's efforts fall short of results satisfying to reason itself.

In some sorts of knowledge the failure of reason can be met by trying again. And even where success is never attained, there is no great harm to either reason or the man reasoning. In general this is true of most speculative knowledges. But there is knowledge in which failure may mean a failure in decisions and choices of action. And failure in choices and action make a man fail. Thus failure in some kinds of knowledge may lead to a moral failure. These kinds of knowledge we shall call "morally related." Assents in such knowledges are influenced in a very special way by the faith. The consideration of this influence will present the third way in which the faith modifies assents in other fields.

By morally related sorts of knowledge I mean those which include the knowledge of their own good use.[21] Some knowledges are neutral regarding their use. Think of mathematics, physics, astronomy. With knowledge of these man can make a guided ballistic missile; but nothing in the knowledge will help its possessor know whether he should make such a missile or, if he has made one, how and when he should use it. How such knowledge should be used is a matter of good or bad choices. This knowledge, neutral regarding good and bad choices, is neutral regarding its own use. There are, however, kinds of knowledge that contain in themselves the knowledge of their own good use. Ethics and moral theology deal explicitly with good choices. Other knowledges supply an understanding of God and man, and are thus necessary as the ground of ethics and moral theology. This knowledge comprises speculative theology and philosophy, history, literature, and political science.[22] History and literature, for example, give a knowledge of man so that a student who understands man (and therefore himself also) through the eyes of Thucydides and Shakespeare knows, in a nonreflective way, some good and bad choices. Also, a student who knows speculative philosophy can understand the central reason why good choices make a man good, just as a student who knows speculative theology can understand how the choice of a limited good, say, to be just in this one business transaction, is really the choice of the unlimited good, God Himself. Such knowledges, therefore, though only implicitly related to actual choices, should be included, along with the explicitly moral knowledges, in the class of morally related knowledges.[23]

The importance of such knowledge for good choices is taken for granted, even by those who could not say what precisely the role of moral knowledge is in good choices. Catholic educators insist that this knowledge should have a privileged place in Catholic colleges. All students are required to give serious consideration to ethics and moral theology, the scientific knowledges of good human choices. As preparation for such study they are also required to ponder the nature of man and his relation to God as known by reason through literature and history and philosophy. The quantitative predominance of such subjects in all degree programs indicates the mind of Catholic educators. But a problem remains. For moral knowledge is, of course, not good choice; it is only knowledge of good choice. The relation of knowledge to good choice will therefore need consideration, though not necessarily here. We shall save it for a later chapter. At present we are discussing the way faith affects assents. We propose to show that the faith has a special influence on assents made in morally related knowledge.

We can see this influence best in explicitly moral knowledge, where the faith leads reason along lines not suspected by reason itself. Consider the problem at the very core af ethics, that of the virtuous man. Reason finds no problem in assenting to the proposition that the virtuous man is happier than the vicious man. But reason has difficulty with the proposition that the virtuous man is happy. That he should be happy seems to be implied by the proposition that the vicious man is not happy. That a man is happy, merely because he is virtuous, does not seem to fit the facts. The facts are that the virtuous man is subject to suffering, just as the evil man is. And at times we find the intolerable situation in which the virtuous man suffers from his very acts of virtue. An example will make this clear. A prudent man decides wisely that his family of five needs a vacation. They go camping. On the return trip, while waiting at a traffic light, their car is rammed from behind by a drunken driver. The prudent man and his three small children are injured; his wife dies of a broken neck. Is this man happy, now or in prospect, with himself and three motherless children in the hospital? He is virtuous, and he is not happy and not soon likely to be so.

There is nothing bizarre about this example. As long as there are men who do not, for whatever reason, obey laws, those who do are subject to suffering from outlaw acts. Moreover, there is always the possibility that chance events, such as lightning, earthquakes, freak accidents, will destroy the happiness of the virtuous man. Both the virtuous and the vicious man are equally subjected to chance events and interference by other men. That the vicious man is unhappy, no matter what the reason, causes no embarrassment to reason. But if the virtuous man is not happy, then reason has run into a dead end. If reason should turn around (that is, decide that vice will produce happiness), it has to give up all pretense of being reason and capitulate to passion. If it stares straight ahead, it can only look into darkness where nothing is clear. There is a third possible alternative. One can, as Socrates did when faced with an unjust sentence of death, turn to conjecture. He put it this way: "Wherefore, O judges, be of good cheer about death, and know for a certainty, that no evil can happen to a good man, either in life or after death."[24] The certainty of Socrates came from his knowledge that the good can never turn out to be the evil. But beyond that he had to rely on conjecture, for he could not know how his death, so patently an irremediable evil, was in some sense also a good for him. To know that requires more facts than reason has at its disposal.

Now faith supplies these additional facts, which are not the consequences of the natures of things man sees—such facts are open to him—but the consequences of God's free promises to man beyond the demands of his nature. The first of these divine facts is that this natural life of man is only a testing ground for a greater life that is beyond what man can conceive. In that life happiness will crown a virtuous life. Here on earth there is only the kind of happiness that can coexist with the precarious state of being tested. Even the virtuous man must pass tests, and he especially needs difficult problems. For good students need hard questions to prove they are good; easy questions test only mediocre students. Grant that this world is a time of testing and that the virtuous need especially searching questions, the unhappiness of the virtuous man, even when caused by the vicious, is not against reason.

The second divine fact is a consequence of the first. If man's happiness is not in this life but is a gift, there is no natural and necessary connection between his actions and his ultimate happiness. By a natural and necessary connection I mean the kind in which the cause accounts for the effect. Put a dime in the vending machine that is working; you get a cup of coffee. Do not put in a dime; no coffee from this machine. Given a fish egg (and conditions for growth), there will be a fish. No fish egg, no fish. These are natural connections between cause and effect. But in moral matters natural connections do not always hold. The prudent father planned a vacation for the good of his family, but the result was anything but good for his family. Still, his action was good and must lead to happiness. Not, however, by a natural and necessary connection. The connection here is one of merit, one set up by the promise of

God. And the promise of God is not that virtuous acts will always make a man happy in this world but that they will always do so in the next and in a way out of all proportion to the action performed. The prudent man will be happy beyond rights, and part of his happiness will derive from the very act that was the occasion of great unhappiness here below.

With these two facts reason is no longer at a dead end. The student, under the guidance of faith, can see that virtuous action is the infallible "means" to happiness. But the infallibility here does not derive from nature, which is always subject to chance events and interference. This sort of guarantee is never more than what holds for the most part; that is, as long as there is no interference. The infallible connection between virtuous action and happiness has the stamp of God's promise on it and shares in His infallibility, to which there are no exceptions. In order to share this infallible connection with happiness, virtuous action must give up any pretense of being the full means or cause of happiness other than the temporary and occasional moments of happiness in this life. Virtuous action does not cause happiness in the next life. God does. But virtuous action is still the only thing that man can perform that will be the acceptable reason why God freely bestows happiness on man.

Besides leading reason, there is a second way that the faith touches assents in moral knowledge. It strengthens assents that reason would otherwise hold with some misgivings. In moral matters a hesitant reason is subject to emotional pressure and is likely to confuse strong preference with good thinking. Consider the contemporary moral issue of divorce and remarriage. That such action is against the moral law is difficult for unaided reason to maintain with surety, especially where brutality seems to exclude true family life. Suppose that the father of six small children is a drunkard who regularly beats his wife and children. The children need a father as well as a breadwinner. The mother needs masculine help to raise the children properly. The man does not even pretend that he wants to reform his life. Why, then, may not the mother divorce him and find, if she can, another husband who will cherish her and the children? The answer unaided reason would give is not hard to see.

But when God steps in and condemns divorce (with remarriage), the student possessed of faith is willing to reexamine the data. He begins to see clearly what before he only vaguely suspected. That is, that divorce is wrong because it undermines the family. Since marriage is a natural society, what improves the family improves men; what hurts the family, hurts men. But what of this one instance of the brutal father? Sympathy—that is, feeling—for the wife and children encourage reason to make an exception in this situation. But reason steps in and asks, "If divorce is evil because destructive of the family and therefore of men, does not your exception say in effect that a good end (good of this wife and these children) justifies an evil means (divorce and remarriage)?" Any reason, with or without faith, can see clearly enough that good ends do not justify evil means. That is, reason now sees clearly, on grounds proper to reason itself, what it saw only vaguely before. Consequently, reason can now make a firm assent that divorce with remarriage is morally wrong, no matter what emotional pressure may here and now suggest as the more "human" solution.

I have used this example of divorce to show how the faith strengthens reason and helps reason do its own work better. I have not attempted to deal fully with the concrete example given. Had I, I would have repeated two truths considered above. These are, first, that the moral good is not good because it satisfies man (though it does) but that man is good because he conforms to the moral good; second, that the relation of human action to man's ultimate happiness (vision of God) is not that his good acts cause happiness but that his happiness will come about only because of good moral actions. At present my only concern has been to show the role of the faith in strengthening reason in moral situations in which reason can easily be swamped by emotions.

The fourth and final way in which faith modifies assents made in the arts and sciences is by humanizing them. In one sense, of course, all arts and sciences are already human and therefore cannot be humanized. That is, they are knowledges of man and as such are human. On this score the faith has nothing to do, when human is opposed to the nonhuman, say, the animal or the angelic. But human can be opposed to the inhuman, and then it means what is perfective or more perfective of men rather than what is destructive or less perfective of men. It is in this setting that we say the faith humanizes assents made in the arts and sciences. A more precise meaning of *humanizes* will appear in the instances of it.

The first instance is that of the Index of Prohibited Books, which we considered above. We indicated that besides its negative aspect it also had a positive aspect, to be taken later. Here is the place where consideration of the Index properly belongs. For its purpose is not to put a stop to assents but to protect the student from what will harm him. The Index is, therefore, not a barrier; it is a shield. A barrier stops one from going some place. It is therefore ultimately negative and restrictive, for it keeps one from acquiring some good. And when one has less good than he could have if the barrier were not in his way, he is less by reason of the barrier. To restrict is to hold one back from the good. A shield, however, only keeps out the harmful. It is therefore ultimately positive and nonrestrictive. For the harmful is such because it deprives one of good, as disease deprives the sick man of health. To keep out disease is one way of keeping the good that is health. A shield (masks, vaccination, narcotic laws, and so on) that protects health is therefore not restrictive but preservative. The same is true of the Index. It is preservative of the student's moral health.

The perfective power of the Index does not consist in the effect it has on student assents. Its power is to be judged by the way it affects the state of possession of such assents. In Chapter 3 we considered fully the importance of the state of possession for both practical knowledge of the virtuous doctor and the speculative knowledge of the just mathematician. There we concluded that acts of good choice made knowledge fully perfective of man by determining the state of possession of such knowledge. Now we are saying that the Index is one of the preservatives of good choices. That is, by excluding matter that encourages certain kinds of bad choices the Index is a shield against these and therefore a preservative of good choices. As such it perfects all assents. For it preserves a state of possession that is perfective of every assent the student has made or will make under its preserving influence.

For our second instance we shall take again the influence of the faith on biology, this time in order to see a more positive role than purification. The biologist's data are living bodies, and his assents deal with their natural constitution and activities. Now let the biologist also have the faith. His biological conclusions, which are clarifications of the data of living nature, are also seen as clarifications of what God has made either personally or through the agency of creatures. There is no question, as we said above and must repeat here, of his faith's entering his biology. This would destroy his biology. What we are describing is what happens when his biology enters his faith. What results is a new vision that destroys neither but strengthens both. His faith gains by seeing in more precise biological detail what faith knows only vaguely and generally. His biology is strengthened by having its conclusions caught up in something greater than itself. Not that his biology is, as biology, made more accurate or certain. If biology is to become more accurate, it must do that for itself. Rather, faith does for the biologist what biology cannot do for him.

What biology, or any natural science, cannot do is justify its full human significance. To say that biology is certain and true knowledge is a partial justification, since man by nature wants to know. But this is hardly a final answer unless one asks how knowledge perfects man. If the justification of biology is only that it satisfies man's curiosity, it hardly deserves the time and attention men give it. Men indeed are curious, but so are rhesus monkeys. What monkeys discover satisfies their curiosity, and that frequently is all that it does. To say that biology's significance is basically the same as the explorations of a monkey before a mirror is to miss something about biology that makes it a human endeavor. One can, of course, appeal to a difference of degree. Curiosity can be intense or halfhearted. It can also be about trifling things or about serious things—the monkey's image in a mirror or the constitution and actions of living bodies. But the difference between trifling and serious objects of curiosity is not a difference of degree of curiosity; it is a difference of things as related to man. The trifling means little to man; the serious, much. That leaves us with the question of why biology means much to man and looking in a mirror means very little.

One answer given to this question and repeated constantly is that through the natural sciences human life is "endowed with new discoveries and powers,"[25] and thus we "render ourselves lords and possessors of nature."[26] In this view natural sciences are primarily tools and have the value of tools. Now, hammers are of no particular value unless you want something hammered. At all other times they are just in the way, as most housewives know. The natural sciences, conceived as means to some other desired good, would have no value when and if they did not supply those other goods. This utilitarian or tool value of natural science, especially emphasized in public life today, is not accepted by all practicing scientists. E. Schrödinger, for example, argues that some natural sciences, such as cosmology and some branches of geophysics, have little practical value. Moreover, he contends that it is extremely doubtful that "the happiness of the human race has been enhanced by the technical and industrial developments that followed in the wake of rapidly progressing natural science." The true value of the natural sciences, along with all other branches of knowledge, "is to obey the command of the Delphic deity: *'gnothi seauton,* get to know yourself.' Or, to put it in the brief, impressive rhetoric of Plotinus (*Enneads* V, 4, 14): *'hemeis de, tines de hemeis';* 'And we, who are we anyhow?' "[27]

To say with Schrödinger that the natural sciences are an integral part of the human endeavor is to make such knowledges valuable in themselves, not merely as tools. Through them man carries on the necessary work of being man. Since his duty is to know himself and the natural sciences help him know himself, they are part and parcel of his living a human life. Still, this answer does not do justice to the natural sciences for the same reason that the Delphic oracle did not do justice to the human problem. Both stop short of the full truth. Experience will soon tell one trying to know himself that the more he knows of himself as if this were the center of reality, the less satisfying is his knowledge. What the oracle should have said was, "Know yourself as caused by God." That is, through knowing yourself see what God is. This is the true human problem, to know God by knowing the things He has made. When any knowledge helps us know God it becomes truly human knowledge.

Faith does this for biology, that it makes it fully human by giving it its (biology's) proper part to play in human life. The human role of biology, its own proper role, is to help man see God in the immensely varied and complicated world of living things. Only biology can do this; yet it cannot do it by itself. For biology has no way to know that God created living beings. Consequently, it has no way to see the living as the work of God. But when faith supplies this knowledge to the mind of a man knowing biology, his very biology can then take its rightful place. It can in its own name and by its own proper excellence forward man in the central endeavor of human existence. In other words, biology without faith is fully biology, since the faith adds nothing biological. But biology without faith is not fully human, since it floats on the surface of the human stream. Something other than biology, the faith, is needed to draw it down into the current where it can add its strength to the flow of human life.

Our third instance of the faith humanizing assents in the arts and sciences is more general than the last. Here we shall consider the general tendency of the mind to run things. Common experience, supplied by all stages of human life, gives ample testimony of this tendency. When the child's mind first begins to function, he begins to have opinions about how his desires are to be satisfied. He begins to want his own way. From this day until his death he continues to want things done according to his plans and his preferences. Some men more than others are insistent on running things, often making a nuisance of themselves. But the most reserved man, if given an opportunity, is apt to tell you what to do, even if he does not expect you to do what he suggests.

This tendency to run things is not a sign of cussedness; it is a sign of intellect or mind. For the mind sees the end or good desired and means to that good. And in seeing this it is conscious of its own excellence of being a runner of things. Without this ability to see ends and means to such ends, freedom in man would be pointless. For freedom can be a cause of action only because it can arrange known means to known ends. Suppose there were no means or that there were means but none arrangeable by man. Freedom would have nothing to do. Likewise, suppose that man did not know what the arrangeable means were; again, freedom would be out of a job. The excellence of being able to run things stems from man's mind, from his intellect, which sees arrangeable means to desirable ends, and from his will to desire ends and means to these ends.

We said above that man is an image of God. We are saying the same now. Man is like God because he can run things. God is provident because He has intellect and will. Because man, too, has intellect and will, he is provident. The difference, of course, is that man's intellect and will must be provident under the providence of God. For man is not merely similar to God in being up to running things. He is also an image. That is, he is similar to God and this similarity is a one-way street. God is not like man. It is only that man is like God. Such is the relation of all images to what is imaged. A man is not like his portrait; the portrait is like him. And the portrait is good or bad, depending on how close its resemblance to the man. The same is true of all images; they are constituted good or bad by their dependence on what they image. The rule or measure is the imaged; the ruled or measured is the image. Thus man, as an image of God, is a good or bad runner of things to the extent that his actions are measured by the providence of God.

Man becomes fully an image of God by his free decisions to become so; otherwise he would not be a runner of things. And this leaves open the possibility of his refusing to image God's providence. He has it within his power to ignore God and try to run things on his own completely. Ignoring God, his intellect and will have no measure or pattern other than the bare tendency itself to run things. All actions will be justified because they are mine; they come from me, and they express myself. The self becomes the center about which all other things swing in orbit. Action becomes self-expression. All goods, such as knowledge and prestige and power, become good because they are self-developing and not the other way round. Man, the individual or the class, becomes the center of all that is, and no place is left for God that is worthy of Him. Man is no longer an image. He is the imaged and all must now reflect his unhinged excellence.

The final step is to protect this self-constituted excellence by a new understanding of the world. The intellect is put to work reassessing the data to be explained. What serves to enhance man's independence is kept and emphasized. Where data do not serve this purpose they are declared meaningless, not data. The whole movement of thought becomes geared to prediction as the central ideal of all knowledge. To know truly is to predict events, natural or human, from their causes. What is predictable is knowable and to that extent controllable by man. What is not predictable to that extent is not controllable. In this way the intellect in principle—though it never succeeds in fact—cuts out the unexpected and the uncontrollable. In principle, too, it succumbs to the temptation proper to a being able to run things; it plays at being God.

That such is the temptation of the human intellect can be seen in the history of Western thought. John Henry Newman saw it.

> I know that even the unaided reason, when correctly exercised, leads to a belief in God, in the immortality of the soul, and in a future retribution; but I am considering it

actually and historically; and in this point of view, I do not think I am wrong in saying that its tendency is towards a simple unbelief in matters of religion. No truth, however sacred, can stand against it in the long run; and hence it is that in the pagan world, when our Lord came, the last traces of the religious knowledge of former times were all but disappearing from those portions of the world in which the intellect had been active and had had a career. And in these latter days, in like manner, outside the Catholic Church things are tending, with far greater rapidity than in that old time from the circumstance of the age, to atheism in one shape or other. What a scene, what a prospect, does the whole of Europe present today! And not only Europe, but every government and every civilization through the world, which is under the influence of the European mind.[28]

Newman said this in 1864, and it could equally well be said today. His thesis is that the intellect, when given its head, tends to deny its status as image of God and declare its total independence. A contemporary economist of national reputation, Kenneth Boulding, points out the same tendency of intellect. "Pride, envy, self-love, self-deceit, self-righteousness, cynicism, frivolousness, and cowardice are common diseases in intellectual circles, and of these the most to be feared is pride, a disease utterly devastating in its ultimate effects, yet so subtle that there seems to be no remedy for it save a simple-hearted daily dependence upon God."[29]

Both Newman and Boulding point out the tendency of the human intellect to cut itself free from God. One other point needs to be added; namely, that this independence dehumanizes man. What is sought on the plea of man's self-perfection undermines his essential human excellence, that of being an image of God. For this independence cuts him off from God. Man thus isolates himself from the only end worthy of him, union with God. He must settle perforce for the end open to animals, a few years of life in this world followed by nothing. And the few years he enjoys have no other purpose than to continue his own species by reproduction and be the means for other spe-cies (for example, cancer cells) to reproduce themselves. If this is what man is thought to be, he has been dehu-manized by being animalized. Any self-glorification which denies man's position of being image of God issues in veiled self-degradation.

The faith blocks each step of this destructive self-glorification of the human intellect. It presents man as a created image of God. Man's intellect and will must there-fore express in providential actions the creaturely status of reflecting the providence of God. Consequently, the hu-man problem is to search for God, not to achieve self-expression or self-improvement by putting self in the place of God. Data may not be culled and slanted to suit man. Data are sacred; they are caused by Him; they ex-press some of His perfection. Data that are impervious to full human understanding or annoying to human prefer-ences are still the work of God and can lead man to God along lines determined by God, not by man. Finally, the life of the mind is to commit oneself by assenting to what is, for in so doing the mind commits itself to knowing God. Channeled by faith's understanding of the world, the mind's tendency to run things can safely be given its head because it will improve man. He will become more a created image of God, his proper and full excellence. His intellectual assents will image the truth of God. His choices, made in the light of such assents, will image the providence of God. In short, he will become more what a man should be; he will become more human.

Briefly now, we can define more precisely the humanizing role of the faith. In each of the instances we presented —the Index of Prohibited Books, biology integrated into the human problem, mind as image of God—the common factor was man's union with God. The Index was a shield to protect existing union (of mind and will) with God. The faith brought biology to its full role of helping man know God. The faith helps the mind remain and grow as image of God. To humanize, taken generally, is to make man more human, to perfect man. Here definitely, to humanize is to strengthen the union of man with God. As a creature, man is made by God, and this is a kind of union with God. As an intellectual creature, man can know his own creaturehood and its consequent demands on his actions. Being a creature that can run things, he must run them as a creature should; that is, as united to God. What unites him to God makes him more a creature. What he does knowingly and freely to increase this union makes him more an intellectual creature, one that is providential after the pattern of Providence itself. Using theological terms, to humanize man is to redeem him, to bring him to his proper status of image of God. In philosophical terminology, to humanize is to make men more rational. In either terminology, human perfection is achieved by a closer union with God.

These, then, are the ways in which the faith, as an existential condition, is operative in college learning. We have considered three sorts of existential conditions: those arising from the student himself, those arising from the teacher teaching, and those from the faith. Obviously, the most important and most pervasive is that of the faith. It humanizes all assents made in the arts and sciences by bringing these into a pattern conducive to union with God. It reinforces assents made in the vital area of morally related knowledges. It makes reason's work easier by supplying insights reason can then exploit for its own purposes. On occasion, it purifies too hasty conclusions in the arts and sciences. Thus the faith is indeed the major single existential condition affecting student assents in a Catholic college. Second to the faith is the instrumental activity of the teacher, teaching what he knows in the way he knows it, with this selection of data and these emphases molded by this intellectual personality. Compared with the teacher or the faith, the state of the student's intellectual development, moral habits, and sense appetites is a less important but still operative existential condition of the assents made by the college student.

CHAPTER 6

RELATION OF SUBJECT

MATTER TO EXISTENTIAL

CONDITIONS OF ASSENT

In order to point up the moral influences operative in a Catholic college, we have distinguished two sets of influences on students making assents. The first derives from the facts, the subject matter taught, the data-problems-

principles-conclusions. These we may call the essential
factors of the act of learning. The second set of influences
derives from the actual circumstances or conditions under
which the data-problems-principles-conclusions come to
the student. These we may call the existential factors of
the act of learning. Having distinguished these two sets
of factors influencing assents, it remains to be seen why
both are crucial to the learning of the student.

In a sense, we have already indicated the importance of
both sets of influences. The mere act of distinguishing
brought out the positive influence of the essential factors
first and then of the existential. But one might argue, at
least theoretically, that the existential factors are relatively unnecessary. Perhaps they might be very important
in a Catholic college. But why in any other college? The
essential factors seem to be sufficient for student assent.
Why not ignore, then, the existential factors as being of
little consequence? To answer this question requires a negative consideration of both factors. Suppose that one factor is emphasized beyond its rightful importance. The
other is necessarily neglected, since part of its rightful
task is taken over by the other. How, then, does this neglect of one or the other affect the student's learning? We
shall consider first the emphasis on essential factors and
the neglect of the existential, then the contrary emphasis
and neglect.

Emphasis on the subject matter to the neglect of existential conditions will mean here the neglect or absence
of faith. The reason for limiting our consideration to neglect of faith is not that we underrate the influences from
the teacher. The reason is that in some ways that is the
only neglect possible. Teachers can hardly not exercise the

influence arising from their personal qualities. They can, however, keep their faith from entering the classroom by positively and consciously excluding what they may happen to possess, or negatively by not possessing the faith. Thus the part of the teacher's influence that can truly be neglected is what comes from the faith of the teacher. Consequently we shall bypass, in this framework of neglect, the existential conditions arising from the teacher and consider only the result of neglect or absence of existential conditions that arise from the faith in both the teacher and the student.

In Chapter 5 we considered the positive influences of the faith on assents. Here we need only recall these in order to see what is lost when the faith is neglected. The arts and sciences, we said, were humanized by the faith. The absence of faith leaves them burdened with their tendency to limit the horizon of man to self and to this life.[1] Again, the sciences, by their very method of specializing in order to know more clearly, encourage intellectual isolation. Without the faith this trend of science has nothing to counteract it but reflective elaborated knowledge, which must lead from the inherent weakness of being only preparatory to science. Finally, extreme specialization easily carries one into intellectual imperialism, more effectively the more successful any one science is. Without the faith the other kinds of knowledge are reduced to being handmaidens, who generally do not tell the empress what she may not wear.

Each of these results—dehumanization, isolationism, imperialism—are varying degrees of partial skepticism. The first renders a student positively skeptical about any truth not obtainable by some human method of knowing. The second produces only negative skepticism, the kind that is satisfied to affirm the truth of some facts and remain neutral towards all others—a position that can arise either from prudence and humility or from calculating pride. When pride is the source of the position, neutrality is only veiled skepticism. The third, imperialism, is aggressive skepticism about any and every fact that is impervious to one method of knowing. Thus partial skepticism is the common factor in each of these results of emphasizing knowledge and neglecting the faith. Strange, is it not, that knowledge can be so pursued that success in knowing results in partial skepticism? But such happens. The reason for the fact needs to be indicated. And to do this requires that we take another look at the nature of knowledge.

We said above that knowledge is a proper account of something. The something is a fact, and facts are what is or can be insofar as they are the object of intellect. Thus being, what is or can be, is the specifier of knowledge, making one knowledge be and be different from another by what it is about. When man is faced in experience with what is, his mind comes into play, and he forms an account of what is.[2] This formed account may be knowledge that something is without being definite about what it is that is. In a dark room, for instance, a man stumbles over something. He is quite sure that the thing is, though he may not be able to say what it is he stumbled over except that it is something in this room. He may go on, because the data contain more than his first account gives, to find out what it is he stumbled over, say, a hassock. And after this act of knowing, he can seek to know why the blasted thing is in the dead center of the room and not near the armchair where it belongs.

On each point a man can be sure; that is, have certain knowledge. It is clear to him that there is something his foot hit, that his foot hit a hassock, that someone did not put the hassock where it belongs. The logical names for the three accounts are a judgment of existence, a concept of an artifact, a causal conclusion. The names are unimportant here. What is important to see is that all three accounts are clear, though not clear about the same facet of the data. Clarity about existence—that something is—is beginning clarity. Without it all subsequent acts of knowledge would be accounts of nothing; they would not be accounts at all. The subsequent acts of knowledge are fuller accounts of what is; each gives man more of the something that is.

For purposes of explanation we need a more significant example than the hassock in a dark room. Newton will supply it. In his *Optics* he makes clear the fact that bodies appear colored by showing the cause of their so appearing. That they appear colored is the original fact, clear as such. But Newton proposes to say why they appear colored.

> These Colours arise from hence, that some natural Bodies reflect some sorts of Rays, others other sorts more copiously than the rest. Minium reflects the least refrangible or red-making Rays most copiously, and thence appears red. Violets reflect the most refrangible most copiously, and thence have their Colour, and so on of other Bodies. Every Body reflects the Rays of its own Colour more copiously than the rest, and from their excess and predominance in the reflected Light has its Colour.[3]

By giving the reason why bodies appear colored Newton has increased our knowledge of colored objects. Not only is there knowledge that bodies appear colored; there is also knowledge of why this must be so. Bodies appear colored and must so appear if they are reflecting refrangible rays of light; and the differences of color in bodies is owing to the predominance of rays of one refrangibility over rays of another refrangibility. In other words, Newton explains the fact of colored bodies by giving the natural cause of color in bodies.

Now for an analysis of what Newton did. The fact of color in bodies presents itself to the human mind as something that has about it more to be known. This "more" stands as an invitation to the mind to discover the mystery the fact contains. There are two paths open to the mind. One is to distinguish precisely the constituents of the fact, indicating its structure, the parts of its structure, the interrelation of these parts to constitute the known structure. Beyond that we can try to find the reason or cause why a fact has the structure we have discovered. Newton took these steps regarding the fact that bodies appear colored. He concluded that color was a property of rays of light, that different colors were due to the different kinds of light rays. The reason why bodies appear colored, according to Newton, is owing to the property they have of reflecting some light rays more than others, so that they appear to have the color of the rays they reflect most copiously. The mystery of colored-appearing bodies has been reduced to knowledge by giving the cause of such appearance.

This example shows the pattern of all knowledge that answers the invitation of mystery. Clearly, knowledge of fact alone is incomplete knowledge. Clearly also, knowledge of structure or pattern of fact is incomplete, though

less incomplete than that of bare fact. Not at all clearly,
but nevertheless true, knowledge of the causes of structure is incomplete too. That is, mystery is an invitation to
more knowledge, but it is not an invitation that ceases.
It is like a standing invitation to a perpetual feast, an invitation that continues even for those who have eaten well.

How does fact present itself to us as an inviting mystery? It does so by presenting itself as being first itself and
then as not being other facts. If there were only one fact,
say one red apple and absolutely nothing else, red apple
would cause no wonder to a mind (that happened on the
scene).[4] To be red would be apple, and to be apple would
be red, and to be would to be red apple. Everything would
fit neatly, with no parts left over. But once there is another
colored thing, say, a green apple, then a mind would become curious. Two mysteries appear. First, how does red
differ from green? Second, how does red or green differ
from apple, since apple is red in one instance and green
in another? To be red is certainly not to be green, and to
be either is not to be apple. Now, if the mind wants to
clarify this mystery it will have to discover what color is.
Thus the facts of red apple and green apple invite the
mind to consider what constitutes the colored.

This, of course, is only one invitation, the one Newton
accepted. The same two colored apples in our present
world contain other mysteries presenting other invitations
that Newton did not accept. For instance, the (chemical)
constitution of the apples, or their (biological) genesis, or
their trade (economic) value, or their value (moral) as
belonging or not belonging to some one. The same data
present such invitations and countless others, including
the ones to discover how there can be two apples, or how

two apples can be one—that is, apple—or how apples can be at all, seeing that they began to be. To answer one of these many invitations, as Newton did, is not to exclude all mystery from the data. At most, it makes progress towards understanding one part of the mystery contained in two colored apples.

Newton's answer to the data as colored is that color is a property of rays of light. One color is distinct from another because of difference in the rays of light and their different combinations. The difference in rays of light is the difference of their wavelengths. Thus Newton can describe the structure of color and go on to say why a body appears colored. Yet even of color and the colored, Newton did not succeed in plumbing all the mystery present. For color is determined by length; the structure of color is length of wave. But length of wave is not the wave; it is only length of it. In other words, color is not light even though light is colored. Very mysterious, indeed, when something both is and is not. Light is not color but is nevertheless colored, and color is not simply light although it is light.[5]

When we consider the causal part of Newton's explanation, we find again that mystery still resides after the explanation. The cause of bodies appearing colored is the quality they have of reflecting rays of certain lengths more copiously than rays of other lengths. Thus we succeed, when we find a cause, in substituting one part of the fact —reflecting bodies—for another part of the fact—colored rays. Given color, you have bodies variously reflecting; given bodies variously reflecting, you have color. The economy of causal explanation is that, once found, the cause can be substituted for the effect; and we can turn our attention to the cause, forgetting about the effect, since it is precontained in its cause. This ideal explanation as operative in the natural sciences is generally stated as prediction. And it is attained, if one wants to know what effects will show up, when light hits a given body. But in the order of knowledge, the ideal of identifying cause and effect never fully succeeds. The cause is not the effect nor the effect the cause, since they remain distinct beings. In Newton's explanation the reflecting body is not the rays it reflects—also the body is not its reflecting even though it is reflecting—and no amount of equating will reduce the stubborn nonidentity of cause and effect. What began as two, color and body, remains as two in spite of the unifying relation of body as reflecting light and color as reflected light. Some unity, some explanation, has been achieved; some not achieved. That is, there is mystery still present even in causal explanation.[6]

The importance of mystery in all reaches of the intellectual life justifies this long analysis of Newton's explanation of colored objects. We discovered that explanation reduces mystery only to find that mystery continued after all our progress. It does so because explained facts are still facts, retaining part of their factuality unexplained. We easily forget this, especially when we hope to encourage college students to move from knowledge held by memory and hearsay up to the level of scientific knowledge. For this reason we praise the thoroughness of the arts and sciences as the culmination of knowledge. We propose to explain facts, as if facts under our tutelage would disappear into their explanations. Understandable as this presentation may be considering all the circumstances, it is not without its danger. The danger is that the student may never quite

see the importance of fact before, during, and after explanation. He may, for instance, think that he can drop the
"flower in a crannied wall" after the poet had his say or
the specimen in the laboratory after the scientist has had
his. He is quite willing to admit that facts need explanation, but thereafter facts can be cast aside for something
better. What he does not see is that facts, even explained
facts, never lose completely their wonder-producing character, their mysteriousness.

Mystery is indeed most clearly present at the inception
of human knowledge, serving as the solid base that gives
footing for progress and justification for seeking more
knowledge. But nothing in the nature of either fact or of
man's mind guarantees that he can dispel all the mystery
resident in facts. Rather, there is good reason to hold the
opposite, when one reflects on man's mind. If man succeeded in dispelling all mystery of fact, his intellectual
life would come to a halt. There would be nothing left for
him to do except perhaps to keep repeating what he
already knew, and thus to become a dreadful bore to himself and others. His mind would have to be judged stag-
nant, not living as a mind lives.

This judgment would be sound too. We have indicated
the double role of mystery in the life of the mind. First,
it reveals itself as what needs explanation and thereby
encourages man to find the causes of fact, giving birth to
the arts and sciences. Secondly, it keeps the mind living
by constantly revealing itself anew so that the work of the
arts and sciences in principle is never finished. Both roles
of mystery must be kept in focus. Otherwise we would
have the strange state of affairs in which mystery would
be the cause of its own destruction. The strangeness is not

in this, that a thing destroys itself; suicides do this often enough to exclude strangeness. What is strange is that something does its very best for self and others at the same time that it does its worst for self and others. It would be like a suicide who expected to live on this earth by killing himself. The same would be true of mystery that did not encourage man's intellectual life. As long as there is mystery, life of the mind is possible; when mystery goes, the mind's life goes with it.

When man forgets this second role of fact as mystery, his desire for the arts and sciences easily blinds him to the real meaning of facts. They become not the inviolable ground of the intellectual life but only the means used to forge his arts and sciences. Facts exist for the sciences, not sciences for the facts. A strange inversion, yet one congenial to the desire to reduce mystery to science, especially when that desire has been strengthened by progress in scientific knowledge. It is still possible, of course, to appeal to facts; but the appeal becomes more and more selective. Only certain facts are desired; namely, those facts that advance a certain kind of scientific knowledge. Those that do not advance the knowledge, those that keep their mystery intact, must be got out of the way by one means or another.

One way to meet the problem of mystery is to say that everything is explainable in principle even though actually not explained at present. That is, there is no such thing as a mystery; there is only a temporarily mysterious state of affairs. This solution is not satisfactory for two reasons. First, it is hardly warranted by the facts that remain mysterious. Secondly, it indicates a hope based on past successes that were themselves achieved by reason of selecting only certain facts. The ones not selected, and not selected because mysterious, remain outside the science and quite possibly outside any science.

A second way to handle mysterious facts is to deny boldly that they are facts. Decree all such facts as meaningless and thus free the mind from any obligation either to explain them or even recognize them as facts. If this way seems too arbitrary, there is a third path open that comes out at the same spot but proceeds along softer ground. Make the troublesome facts subjective. Beauty, for example, in a statue or painting is a mysterious fact. Make beauty (of the artifact) subjective and say that beauty is really in the viewer. Once beauty becomes subjective there is no longer any necessity or possibility of saying anything about it beyond indicating its subjectivity. Everyone knows there is no accounting for taste, which is taken to mean that a subjective "fact" is not really a fact at all. Besides beauty, there are other mysterious facts that are likely candidates for being elected subjective, such as morality and religion and, at times, even knowledge itself.

Now, each of these attempts to exclude mystery is nothing but partial skepticism. We said that it would seem strange that emphasis on subject matter—emphasis on knowledge, that is—would lead to skepticism. It does, though, as we have shown, when the desire for science overpowers our respect for facts and the mystery of facts. When the desire for knowledge obscures the ground of knowledge, it is normal to identify subject matter and fact. And this identification is equivalent to denial of mystery because subject matter is fact selected because we can, or at least expect to, explain it. Thus unrelieved emphasis on subject matter tends to partial skepticism by denying the mysterious in facts. What effectively stops this tendency is the presence of the faith, as an existential condition, in the minds of the teachers and students of the arts and sciences. Conscious of divine mystery and the place of mystery in their faith, they are not likely to exclude mystery from the facts of nature. They neither deny directly nor indirectly—make subjective—what cannot be explained. That nature has mysteries of its own is to be expected, seeing that the God of nature is mysterious.

Besides partial skepticism, which is the effect in the area of speculative knowledge, of unrelieved emphasis on subject matter, there is a by-product in the area of practical knowledge. By-products arise from a process that is achieving its purpose and are generally most distinctive when the process is working most perfectly. Here, too, the by-product of emphasis on subject matter is most distinctive and well-formed when speculative knowledge is at its perfect or scientific level.

The proper excellence of scientific knowledge is its necessity. The kind of clarity sought is the kind that sees not only that so and so is true but that it must be true. Such necessity comes, of course, from the object and the way it is known. Recall that speculative knowledge is such because of its dependence on the object that is. If the object has necessity in it, the knowledge shares in this necessity; if the object has no necessary factors in it, it is not a scientific object. The certainty of physics, for instance, arises from the fact that bodies or particles must act the way they do. Since these actions are held to necessary probability patterns, the knowledge of such actions can have the same necessity. So it is in all speculative knowledge.

The ideal is to know what is necessarily so, in the present or in the future. Obviously, men who seek such knowledge must develop ideals of guarded caution that demands constant checking and revision lest they accept as necessary what is not strictly so. Consequently, everything not evident must be proved to the satisfaction of any competent man. And proved knowledge, the standard of top speculative knowledge, easily becomes the ideal of all knowledge, especially when such knowledge takes up most of one's time. This constant predominance of scientific knowledge pushes the student, especially the good student, to conclude that speculative knowledge is the paramount good of man; that all knowledge worthy of the name must be like good speculative knowledge.

This by-product of overemphasis on speculative knowledge is a new kind of imperialism. Instead of one speculative knowledge lording it over other kinds of speculative knowledge, speculative knowledge lords it over practical knowledge by demanding the same conditions for both. Practical knowledge is not the same as speculative knowledge, does not have the same characteristics. One deals with objects and the other with ends. The necessity proper to objects—what must be—is not the same as the necessity proper to ends—what ought to be. Nor is the posture of the knower before an object the same as his posture before an end. Guarded caution and constant checking and revision are essential for achieving good speculative knowledge. The same caution and revision regarding an end stops practical knowledge before it gets started. Ends demand commitments, not continuing cautious appraisal and revision. To submit ends to the treatment proper to objects debilitates the sources of activity. This enervation is not one arising from lack of interest, as seen in the caricature of the absentminded professor. Anyone, not only the professor, can ignore the inconsequential. The debilitation I speak of is one that impedes action where action is demanded and is given full attention. When one demands for his choices the same certainty he demands for his scientific assents, he is likely to find himself on the fence when the good and bad have taken sides. He may retreat into the more congenial world of abstractions and pride himself on his scientific indifference. He may also look with profound disdain on the stupidity of the good but uninformed persons who fail to understand fully the complicated issues involved in practical problems.[7] Whatever may be the individual's rationalization, paralysis of will sets in when an end is treated as if it were an object.

Paralysis of will is generally preceded by a failure in knowledge of what choices should be made. This prior failure can also be traced to the spell of scientific knowledge. The very ideal of this kind of knowledge is what is proved absolutely and certainly. When the ideal is not attained, one talks of disputed opinions or of provisional and doubtful positions. Now the absolutely proved propositions in any one science are not many. Yet this paucity of perfect knowledge causes no hardship to the patient thinker; it encourages him to work more seriously at his investigations. The speculative thinker can, with a show of grace, live with disputed opinions about nature and things, no matter how unsatisfactory these opinions may of necessity be.

Suppose, however, he brings this same attitude into the field of morally related knowledges, the knowledges that deal with the correct choices man should make. In these

knowledges, how many propositions can be proved absolutely and certainly? The ones that cannot must, following
the pattern set in speculative knowing, be classed as disputed opinions. Only here the disputed opinions are about
the nature of man and the actions perfective of man. To
hold to neutrality on such questions is to be unable to say
what is the good and what the bad for man. In speculative
knowing unresolved opinions are no skin off the thinker's
nose. In practical knowledge unresolved opinion may skin
him alive. He may find himself naked before issues that
most demand the armor of whatever certainty the facts
will permit.

This last point can best be shown in an example. Bertrand Russell has argued that in philosophy a "healthy
relativism" (where one is not absolutely certain of any
truth) goes hand in hand with liberalism and democracy.
On the other side of the fence, "philosophical dogmatism"
(where one is certain of some philosophical truths) con-
sorts with intolerance and ultimately with political tyr-
anny. Here is the way he is forced to face the actualities
of Stalin and Hitler in *Philosophy and Politics*:

> If it is certain that Marx's eschatology is true, and that as
> soon as private capitalism has been abolished we shall all
> be happy ever after, then it is right to pursue this end by
> means of dictatorships, concentration camps, and world
> wars; but if the end is doubtful or the means not sure to
> achieve it, present misery becomes an irresistible argument
> against such drastic methods. If it were certain that with-
> out Jews the world would be a paradise, there could be no
> valid objection to Auschwitz; but if it is much more prob-
> able that the world resulting from such methods would be
> a hell, we can allow free play to our humanitarian revulsion
> against cruelty.[8]

All that Russell can work with is a "much more probable" opinion, which of course leaves as a probable opinion that political concentration camps and mass murder chambers are good and right political means. Russell's position may be the best that he can give, but is it good enough for men to live by?

This question has been answered by Etienne Gilson, commenting on Russell's statement above.

In short, Lord Russell invites us to live in a society where democracy is safe because there is high probability that Marx and Hitler are wrong, although there remains a possibility that they may be right. Would we not feel safer in a society where it was understood that truth cannot be proved by burning any number of heretics at the stake; that dictatorships, concentration camps and world wars are criminal in themselves; that even if the murder of a single Jew sufficed to turn the world into a paradise, there would be no justification for killing him? I do not know if the world is destined ever to become a paradise, but the safest way to bring it nearer to being one would be strictly to obey the divine law: "Thou shalt not kill." Or else, if we prefer philosophy to religion, let us repeat with Kant: no human being should ever be used as a means to any end, because he himself is an end. This means not a single person, for any political reasons or under any political circumstances. Quite recently, Russell stated as the first of his ten commandments to save society from fanaticism, "Do not feel absolutely certain of anything." My own question now is: In what type of a society will there be more chance for political tolerance to prevail? Is it in a society whose leaders are not "absolutely certain" that mass murder is not sometimes permissible? Or is it in a society whose leaders feel absolutely certain, with Kant, that political murder is a crime? Against political fanaticism, a philosophical relativism is the weakest possible protection.[9]

Bertrand Russell defended relativism as a philosophical position. But whether one defends the position by argument or is merely caught with the consequences of extending the ideals of speculative science to practical knowledge makes little difference in the final outcome. Both positions leave man unable to meet his most serious problems, for he finds himself in principle unable to take sides with full conviction. That he is protected against siding with bad men may be a consolation. But this consolation is illusory when it becomes obvious that he is not on the side of good men either. What such a man needs is to realize that the existential conditions of knowledge also have a part to play in the life of mind. Scientific knowing, by itself, is sufficient neither for knowing—it encourages practical skepticism—nor for directing action—it enervates the springs of action.

Now we turn to the third effect of overemphasis on subject matter in learning. It is that exclusive concentration on subject matter leaves the existential conditions of learning free to operate without let or hindrance. When existential conditions are recognized and examined, their influence can possibly be ordered and modified to serve the learning process. When they go unexamined, they are not thereby less operative. If anything, they are more operative for not being kept in the open and more likely to shove the learner onto a siding because reason never gets a chance to hold him to the main line. Existential conditions are always present in acts of learning from a teacher. If both student and teacher recognize their presence, both student and teacher can see that they aid, or at least do not interfere with, true learning. When they go unexamined, strange results can be expected.

An example of this last point can be seen in the controversy over "irreligion" in the public schools; that is, public grammar and high schools. In the early 1950's the problem was raised in these terms, "Are the public schools godless?"[10] Now the problem is generally stated in the setting of "the moral and spiritual values in public schools." Public-school officials resented the criticism that the public schools were godless, as if in some way they were accused of teaching atheism or were positively hostile to religion. Were the criticism so understood, it would mean that the subject matter was inimical to religion. This is certainly an unjust criticism. But the criticism could just as well be grounded on the existential conditions of learning. For example, an editorial in a national weekly magazine accused one religious group of dodging "the more serious issue that the religious 'neutrality' of the public schools has become a form of irreligion."[11] One answer to this criticism began: "In an editorial in a recent issue of a magazine with a national circulation, a point of view toward public schools is presented that is being advanced with increasing frequency. In essence the editorial asserts that the public schools are irreligious. This term is not used to mean simply *not* religious, but rather in the sense of showing a disregard for or a hostility to religion."[12] The "hostility" of the answer and the "neutrality" of the editorial might seem to be separated by a broad line. Such would be the case if one read both terms as applying to the subject matter taught in public schools. But when the two terms are read as applying to existential conditions, the line between them is very fine. How fine can be shown by expanding somewhat the argument indicated in the editorial.

This expanded argument is mine, since I do not propose to say what the editor had in mind. Here is the argument. Neutrality of the public schools regarding religion means first of all that religion is not one of the subjects taught. "Religion" in this proposition applies both to the truths held by any one religious body—say, Jewish, Catholic, Protestant—as well as to religion in general. The religious tenets of any one group of citizens could hardly be taught legally if the present interpretation of the First Amendment is at all accurate. Religion in general, composed of those truths common to all faiths, might conceivably be taught under the American constitution. But no one would be pleased with it. Parents who did not want their children taught any religion could object effectively. And those with religious beliefs would be even more opposed to such teaching, which would confuse their beliefs with some amorphous common religion.[13] This opposition to common religion need not be grounded in sectarian intransigence. The nature of religious belief as a personal commitment rules out general abstractions, which are objects, not ends. Thus public schools cannot teach general religion and may not teach any one religious faith.

My second proposition is this. Where religion is not taught and other subjects are taught, religion necessarily has a negligible status relative to the subjects taught. And those latter represent the major task of the pupil's working day, just as the school stands as the director of all his important formal learning experiences during the school week. What the school expects the pupil to learn must be considered as important for the life of learning. The opposite would also seem to be true; namely, that what is not taught in school is not considered important for the life of learning. No one need tell the student this. Few, if any, public-school officials would agree that religion is of no importance to learning in school. Yet the existential condition—that religion is not taught—would encourage the student to take for granted what the conditions of his learning do make factual, that religion is not necessary to the life of learning. The existential condition, of neglecting to teach religion, is itself "teaching" what no one perhaps planned to teach, that religion is negligible in the life of learning.[14]

The conclusion of this argument is that neutrality to religion in the public schools equates religion with the negligible—which is certainly one way of showing "disregard for" and one way in which those "hostile to" religion could be expected to act. Merely because there are other ways of showing disregard and hostility does not keep this one of neglect from being so designated.

My purpose in raising the question of the public schools and religion is not to enter the lists of this continuing controversy. I bring it in here to show that even if one concentrates on subject matter in teaching and learning, and gives no thought to existential conditions, this by no means excludes the influence on student assent that comes from existential conditions. The existential condition of neutrality to religion affects learning in public schools. And it works most effectively when both teacher and student are not aware of its influence on their teaching and learning. Thanks to the present controversy, public-school officials and professional educators are discovering the need to do something about the existential conditions in public schools relative to religion. Under the rubric of "moral and spiritual values" they are exploring the possible lines of

action compatible with the present interpretation of the
First Amendment to the Constitution. Some speak about
the "school climate";[15] some refer to the religious faith of
teachers;[16] some speak of teaching "much useful informa-
tion about religious faiths, the important part they have
played in establishing the moral and spiritual values of
American life, and their role in the story of mankind . . ."[17]
Notice that all these suggestions deal with the existential
conditions of learning, even the last. On the surface "facts
about religion" might be taken as part of subject matter.
They are, but not the subject matter of religion. Facts
about the importance of the natural sciences in our culture
are not natural science; they are history or sociology, just
as facts about religion are.

We can summarize now the results for learning when
existential conditions, especially the presence of faith, are
not given proper attention. First there is the tendency of
subject matter to encourage partial skepticism by its specialization that results in isolationism and possibly imperialism. Moreover, scientific subject matter tends to partial
skepticism by its demand for the one kind of clarity that
excludes mystery from facts. The second result, growing
out of the ideals of scientific knowledge, was the debili-
tating effect of demanding that all knowledge, even practical and morally related knowledge, must exhibit the
necessary character proper to scientific knowledge. This
demand has two consequences. One seems to justify not
taking sides when sides should be taken; the other leaves
a person with only probable opinions to meet the major
decisions of personal and political life. The third result is
that existential conditions, given no attention because
subject matter was overemphasized, easily exert an influ-

ence out of proportion to their importance, becoming more influential precisely from not being noticed and examined. So much for the effects of overemphasis on subject matter and the consequent neglect of the existential conditions of the assent made.

Consider now the other end of the spectrum, where existential conditions are emphasized and subject matter is neglected. Again, one factor in learning will have to do the work proper to both acting together and is therefore condemned to failure from the start. But failure here always has an anti-intellectual flavor to it. Neglect of existential conditions in learning pushes the learner towards partial skepticism. Neglect of subject matter pushes the learner towards an anemic intellectual life.

The reason why existential conditions, when overemphasized, lead to intellectual anemia is found in a human drive that is thwarted. Students, like everyone else, want certainty. But subject matter superficially presented has no power to justify assents that are firm and certain. The data will not be broken down to isolate the precise object being considered; the principles used will either be left so vague and general as to be more ambiguous than the data or not be seen as applicable to the data to be understood; the conclusion will consequently not be a true conclusion. This neglect of subject matter leaves the reasoning process with no proper guarantee of its validity. The only proper one is intrinsic, the known involvement of the conclusion in the premises fully understood. It is relatively easy to see what the data and principles are; it is even easy to see some vague connection between the conclusion and these premises. What is hard to see and what is never seen when subject matter is considered superficially is that this conclusion must follow if these premises are true. Not just any involvement will do but only the kind that fully justifies the reasoning process, since one sees that these premises could not be true unless this conclusion followed from them or that this conclusion would be unthinkable unless these were its premises. Without this kind of intrinsic guarantee for a reasoned assent the student will have to cast about to find some extrinsic causes of his assent.

He will, too. His drive for certainty will take care of that. No student proposes to settle for guesswork, even when he is doing it. Neither he nor anyone else considers ignorance an ideal. Rather than not know he will assent to some conclusions for extrinsic reasons when the intrinsic ones are not open to him. There are, of course, plenty of extrinsic reasons to hand, such as textbooks and teachers and bull sessions, not to mention the sound of one's own voice winning a cheap victory. In a Catholic college the dominant extrinsic reason for assent, especially in morally related knowledge, is the faith. It is dominant for two reasons. One is its inherent excellence; the other is its constant presence. For students may change teachers, and certainly they may change textbooks; they are not likely, though, to change their faith.

Given the human drive to certainty in the presence of overemphasized existential conditions of learning that result in neglecting subject matter, you have the recipe for anemia of the intellect. So far we have given only the main ingredients of this recipe. The rest of the present chapter will be devoted to a clearer description of them. Our interest will be concentrated on the faith as an existential condition. We shall not consider the influence of the teacher (and his textbook) for the same reason as given in the first part of the chapter, the reason that teachers in most circumstances have their full influence on student learning. Thus some special exaggeration of the teacher's influence is not likely, except where his faith supplies for his own understanding of subject matter. This last situation will be subsumed under consideration of the faith as an exaggerated existential condition of student assent. As for the conditions set up by the student's personality, we shall consider one such case to show how it leads to intellectual anemia. It is possible, of course, for one scientific knowledge to be an exaggerated existential condition of other knowledge.[18] Such, however, is really the result of overemphasis of subject matter, which has been considered sufficiently in the first part of this chapter. We shall therefore limit consideration to what happens when the faith or the student's personality controls the act of learning.

As an example of the latter consider the result of over-operative good will. In adult life a person burdened with more good will than sense is called a "do-gooder." He is so taken up with the desire to cure the ills of the world that he fails to find out what the precise facts are he hopes to change. His only resource is good will, so that he rushes out to fix what he does not understand. A disciplined mind would have supplied the knowledge of critical facts and the kind of vision necessary to moderate and direct his energy according to some sensible plan offering some hope of success. Lacking such intellectual discipline and impatient of acquiring it now, his chances of success are slim. Even his accidental successes are not his but are the result of chance. The more common result will be that he undoes more than he fixes. As Cardinal Newman said, in a slightly different context, "There is no greater calamity for a good cause than that they [the intellectually undisciplined] should get hold of it."[19]

In student life, too, one can try to substitute good will for intellectual discipline. One form of this substitution is on an obvious level. It happens when a student thinks he knows merely because he puts in time studying. Teachers hear this plaint frequently, "Why did I fail? I studied hard for this exam." Since this is an expression of discontent rather than an expression of misunderstanding, it is easy enough to correct. Once the student finds out that examinations test what he knows, not how long he studied, the mistaken view is righted.

A more serious substitution takes place when the student lays down the moral good as the condition for the true. For now he is not confusing the good with the true, which is always a temptation when strong desire rushes intellect off its feet. Rather, he is taking an intellectual position about the nature of truth. Facts, in order to be the object of intellect, must also be morally good in the sense of edifying. Thus his criterion for the true is not merely what is but what is and at the same time is morally good. Facts that do not appear edifying can simply be ignored as having no intellectual future. The ones that appear edifying gain his immediate attention as what can yield truth. An instance of an edifying doctrine is that man has a spiritual soul. Presented with such, the student of good will accepts it gladly. His positive proof or reason for accepting such a doctrine is its many consequences, such as man's superiority to animals, personal responsibility, a future life—all edifying. Negatively, his reason is that if man does not have a spiritual soul the logical consequences are the opposite of edifying.

Being right for the wrong reason may be better in practical life than being wrong; but in the intellectual life such is not the case. The student who is wrong can be shown where he is wrong and is teachable. The student who is right for the wrong reason may well not be teachable. Since he holds the same conclusion as the teacher, he sees nothing to learn. Reasons are given him different from the ones he was accustomed to use. But this fact leaves him intellectually indifferent. His own reasons were acceptable because of the conclusion; and since his conclusion has not changed, why get in a stew about other reasons? The conclusion is not more edifying for having other reasons. Moreover, with such a student there is no question of better reasons. He could not distinguish one as better than another because he does not understand what a reason does for a conclusion. The criterion for his assents is not facts grounding reasons that make evident the truth of the conclusion; his criterion is the moral implications of the conclusion.

Such a student, with an overoperative good will, has no sympathy with the ideals of scientific knowledge. Strict proof of anything would appear to him as unintelligible hairsplitting, minutiae that teachers think up in their spare time. In a college where true learning is played down—either positively, by making it secondary, or negatively, by not demanding more than superficial generalities—he would find a prominent niche, even basking in the reputation of being a superior student. But in a college dedicated to the best knowledge possible, he would be miserably—and to him unaccountably—out of place.

Our consideration of the effects of an overoperative good will in the life of learning should not be taken as a condemnation of good will. Recall that knowledge as fully perfective of man demands absolutely the condition that the man's will be good. In students, too, good will is top excellence and hard to come by. In younger students it is charming, even without knowledge. But as the student advances in age and has had the opportunity to learn well and precisely, the presence of mere good will is a charm that is hard to take. He has let his good will stand as the dictator of truth. The result is blindness, which consists in not seeking what is or why it is.

Our second example of an overemphasized condition will be the faith. Here we do not mean the faith as developed to the level of theology. So understood, the faith is scientific subject matter, which, if overemphasized, leads to intellectual imperialism, treated above. Our interest here is the faith as an existential condition that is itself not a scientific subject matter. When faith at this level dominates the act of learning as an overoperative existential condition, it sets up the terms on which all knowledge must exist in this mind. Whatever enters must pass this doorkeeper, receiving his stamp of approval. Or better, the faith is like colored glasses that give the same color to every ray that passes through them.

The "color" proper to the faith is authority. That is to say, this knowledge is held on the word of another. In divine faith, the middle term, or reason for the assent, is always "God said so." In human faith the middle term is "a man says so." Faith, whether divine or human, has a rightful place in human knowledge when the following situation obtains. One person knows what is; a second person, who does not know what is, wishes to share, without proving, the first person's knowledge. He does it by faith, if at all. Divine faith and human faith coincide in this, that both are knowledge certified by the word of another.[20] If I have never seen San Francisco, ultimately I will have to take someone's word for it who has been there, just as Christ told Nicodemus he would have to do regarding the kingdom of God (John 3:13). Again, if a researcher who knows little about physics wants to use the knowledge of the physicist, he will have to invoke authority; and his borrowed knowledge is held on faith. That the physicist held the same knowledge as science in no way touches the researcher's knowledge of the same facts. One cannot appeal to what "physics says." The only sayers are scientists, and they say what they see for themselves. When anyone, scientist or nonscientist, says what he does not see but what others do, he is using faith, grounding his knowledge on the integrity of the men he borrows from.

The extraordinary development of the natural sciences might have encouraged men to think that the extension of the sciences would be attended by diminishing faith among men. Such has not been the result. If anything, the growth in the natural sciences has increased the area of faith for the generality of men. All nonscientists must rely on faith to appropriate the conclusions of the scientists. Even scientists when out of the field of their own competence must rely on the word of other scientists. There is nothing wrong with this. It flows naturally from two facts: (*a*) that no one man knows all that other men know; (*b*) that it is not always necessary to redo what others have done well. There is room for criticism, however, when such men forget that they, like everyone else, depend on human faith. Paul Weiss puts the criticism clearly: "A world of experts, each concerned with asserting only what he himself really knows, is a world of men who must accept without cavil what the other experts offer to them as data, method, outcome—or it is a world of separated items, cut off from all else. Such experts practice what none is willing to preach. On the one side they accept nothing but what they can themselves certify, and on the other they embrace with equal confidence that which they confessedly could not possibly certify."[21]

The role of faith, then, in human knowledge is to make it possible for men to share, without having to prove, the knowledge of others. The reasons for such sharing are many. Mere convenience may justify acts of faith in matters of little significance, such as who took whom out to dinner. Practical impossibility of knowing for oneself will justify faith in more important matters, such as the national population figures supplied by the Bureau of the Census. The natural impossibility of knowing for oneself makes faith the only way to know some truths; for example, the divine mysteries of the Trinity and the Incarnation. Mystery, as we used it in the first part of this chapter, can mean simply what is not known. It can also be used in its original Greek meaning, a known secret. When we speak of divine mysteries the word "mystery" is used in this second sense to mean the secrets of divine wisdom, truths proper to God's knowledge and not open to creatures unless God tells them. Sometimes we speak of unknown facts as secrets; for example, the secrets of nature. But since nature in this sense is not a knower, these are strictly not the secrets of nature but only natural facts not yet known by some or by all men. In principle they are knowable by man; in fact they are not known. There is no possibility of faith in such secrets because nature, so conceived, is not a knower whose word one can accept. What one man knows can be a secret, and another can have faith in this. But such is faith only in fact, not in principle. The secrets of God are in fact and in principle not open to man naturally. These truths must be given to him, either by way of the word of God or by God giving Himself as an object for the human mind.

In divine faith the appeal to authority, the word of God, is not just a convenience that saves the time and effort of redoing what has already been done. Appeal to the word of God is the way God has offered men knowledge of some secrets of God. Now, what is true of the mysteries of God is not true of the "mysteries" of creatures. There is no reason ahead of time why God could not, if He wished, personally reveal natural as well as strictly divine truths. Both sets of truths could be held on faith. But the natural truths could be certified by reason as well as the word of God, while divine mysteries cannot be certified by reason. This difference between what is directly revealed and what must be so revealed if men are to know it, will appear rather pointless to one who makes the faith an overoperative condition of all his knowledge. Why bother about what is known by faith and reason, what only by faith? Any truth that enters a man's mind will have to be certified by authority, even when backed only by reason. The authority, of course, need not be always God's clear words. It may also be any of those who are on God's side. Indirectly their authority is backed by Him, since He is truth and those on His side speak the truth and therefore in a sense speak for God.

This dominance of faith in learning may seem to exalt faith at the expense of reason. What actually happens is that the two become so confused together that they become one single source of knowledge. Faith is not reserved for the mysteries of God. It gets caught up in the proper work of reason. At the same time, reason gets caught up in the proper work of faith. And the intellectual punishment for this confusion is not merely that one loses respect for reason, bad as this is. The punishment is that one loses the ground for respecting either faith or reason.

What happens to faith is that it gets cut off from mystery. Let divine mystery be scrambled with natural knowledge, so that one does not know where reason's conclusions stop and mystery begins. Mystery then turns up as proved from natural reasoning. Consider this line of thinking. One can prove the existence of God as a personal creator. One can prove that the Gospels are credible. The next step is to show that Christ said in the Gospels that He was God. If on the showing of reason one can assert these three propositions, can he conclude from reason that Christ is divine, the Son of God? All you get from reason is that He said He was divine. If you wish to go further and affirm that He is divine, you will have to rely on His word; and that is faith. But any college student who scrambles faith and reason will be certain that he can prove the divinity of Christ. He walks by reason from facts straight into the heart of a divine mystery, never suspecting that his naive enthusiasm for that revelation is destroying the very core of the revelation he loves. Had he recalled the words of Christ—"No one can come to me unless he is enabled to do so by my Father" (John 6:66)—he need not have made this mistake, though he would hardly be in a position to understand Christ's words when he read them. Having lost the distinction between faith and reason, he has also lost the distinction between reasoned conclusion and divine mystery. And without divine mystery there is no absolute need of faith.

Reason, too, suffers in the confusion. It becomes accustomed to acting with no clear understanding of what justifies its acts of knowing. In the example above, reason thinks it proves the divinity of Christ when in fact its conclusion is one of faith. And the problem here is not merely that faith is introduced. The problem is that the student did not know he had introduced faith. He thought that his premises from philosophy and history would establish the conclusion that Christ was divine. A mistake in reasoning is one thing, but a mistake with no means of seeing it is a mistake is another and more serious defect. That is the predicament of one who thinks he proves the divinity of Christ.

To such a mind the ideal of scientific knowledge becomes impossible, just as it does for the mind that insists on truth's being edifying—and for the same reason. A person is willing to affirm conclusions as certain when the premises are not certain or when the premises, though certain, do not imply the conclusion. Such a person's knowledge will lack the precision necessary for certainty, and he will never see the principles that could give clear light to certain conclusions. His highest intellectual work will be opinion at its best and guesswork at its worst. But the excellence of scientific knowing will be beyond such a mind.

Of course, a student could be so taken up with the truths of faith that he would willingly forego all scientific knowledge. But in this he would be giving up more than he realizes, since the faith itself can be developed to the scientific level of theology. Starting with the truths of faith as first principles that constitute true and certain premises, the human mind reasons to conclusions certified by these premises. The same truth may also be certified directly by faith in a case where it is a fact and not a conclusion. What theology can do is to certify this truth by reason enlightened by faith, presenting it as conclusion derived from premises. For example, Christ said in the Garden of Olives: "And yet, not as I will, but as thou [Father] willest" (Matt. 26:39). Theology would reason from the premises that Christ is truly God and truly man; therefore there must be two wills in Christ. What is known by faith is also known scientifically; that is, through its cause, though the reasoning is wholly within faith. This is theology, *fides quaerens intellectum*, faith using reason to understand its God-given truths as well as it can. It seeks to make these as intelligible to man as possible. One highly prized factor of intelligibility is the cause why a thing is so. Seeking this kind of knowledge about the data of faith issues in scientific theology.[22]

The student mind in which faith is overoperative is not up to learning scientific theology. He has no patience with the mental effort necessary to see why premises do demand conclusions. In a way this is understandable, for he has never experienced a sharp act of reasoning. He has never looked at data long enough or taken the time to grasp principles as self-evident and thus has never seen, and possibly does not suspect, the necessary relation of premises to conclusion. Hence he has never experienced the certainty of knowing well. In place of evidence he substitutes some other criterion of certainty; often enough it is familiarity. What he has always heard is ground enough for his opinions. He is quite content to solve a theological problem presented in college with a catechism answer memorized in grammar school.

This block to reasoned knowledge is itself bad enough, especially in a student whose very life of relative leisure should be justified by his learning something well. Yet this lack of knowledge is not his only loss. What happens to his mind is a more permanent loss. Had he learned as he ought, his mind would have acquired a constant, easy readiness to do good thinking about this or that subject. As it is, having not learned anything well, his mind has acquired a constant, easy readiness to bring in the faith where it has no business to be. Before college he might have slipped and missed the point. Now he can do it with assured ease and proficiency.[23] Also, with illusions of grandeur. For before he did not know and knew it. Now he does not know and thinks he does. Of course, the slow student is not tempted to such illusions. His temptation is to be a follower and repeat as faithfully as he can what he hears others say—a product that hardly justifies the energy and expense of carrying on a college.

It is not too surprising that overemphasis of the faith in learning produces an atmosphere of anti-intellectualism. Where such emphasis is placed, it is justified more by virtue than knowledge. In the name of moral virtue, the faith and other edifying conditions of learning are encouraged to take over the work of reason. They take over what they cannot manage.[24] The result is a student improved in neither knowledge nor moral virtue. Not in knowledge, because he has learned nothing properly and fully and will therefore never, thanks to his schooling, carry on any other than an ersatz intellectual life. Nor in moral virtue, because his virtue is not grounded on solid understanding, and he is left with no stable reason for the faith that is in him. Whatever the justification of a Catholic college is, it must be in some sense to put faith at the service of knowledge so that good knowledge can then be put at the service of the faith. Seedy knowledge will not serve the faith; it only makes the faith share its own shabbiness.

Existential conditions, whatever they are, cannot do the work of subject matter, whatever it is, just as subject matter not morally related cannot supply its own existential conditions. Yet both are necessary, and a balance between them is necessary. To achieve this balance both factors of learning need constant attention. Neglect of existential conditions puts assents to subject matter at the mercy of hidden but operative influences, ending in partial skepticism. Neglect of subject matter converts assents into judgments based on preference, ending in anti-intellectualism. Between the two sorts of neglect, there is little to choose. Both end in similar results, in prejudgments not based on facts. Some may prefer, if they are to be wrong, to be wrong owing to one rather than the other neglect. But even this is itself a prejudgment, based on temperament and training.

In general, teachers and students at a secular college seem to prefer to emphasize subject matter and take their chances on neglecting the existential conditions, especially those arising from religious faith. They thus place themselves in the constant temptation of letting subject matter usurp the work proper to one existential condition. This will not come off without its full share of prejudgments, unless perception and vigilance are operative. By contrast, the teachers and students of a religiously committed college prefer to place themselves in the constant temptation of letting the existential condition of their faith usurp the proper role of subject matter. This will not come off without its full share of prejudgments, unless perception and vigilance are operative. Thus both types of colleges have their strong and weak points. But a religious college does have this advantage, that it can afford to admit its source of weakness and can, if it wishes, meet its temptation head on. The secular college, however, tends to deny that its lack of faith is a weakness. If it does so, it has no public way of meeting a temptation that on principle it does not recognize. But the imbalance between subject matter and the condition of faith is there and is a defect.

CHAPTER 7

REASONED ASSENTS

AND

MORAL CHOICES

The reader will be aware, perhaps only vaguely and generally, that something is lacking from our analysis of college teaching and its relation to morality. No doubt the elements we have emphasized are of paramount importance. They are these: the nature of reasoned assents as necessarily derivative from, and dependent upon, the data and the principles of those data; the existential conditions of the possession of such assents; the necessary balance between the reasoned assents and the conditions of their possession. Patently those elements are the elements that must be considered. Yet there is something lacking in the results, like a jigsaw puzzle on a surface so uneven that the parts do not fit snugly. The picture can be recognized, but it lacks cohesion of parts.

What is needed is to understand the relation of taught knowledge to moral choices. The three factors we have analyzed are themselves either knowledge or the conditions of knowledge; not one of them is choice, to which moral virtue is ordered. Even the knowledge of good choices, which is ethics or moral theology, is not itself choice and is therefore not the result of moral virtue or the acts that flower in moral virtue. Choices, not knowledge, are the sure ground and the achievement of virtue. If our analysis has taken up its time mainly with knowledge, we must show that this knowledge does have something to do with choices. Otherwise, we have no right to talk about knowledge and moral virtue in teaching.

There is a second reason, and one that arose from our analysis of the perfective power of knowledge, that invites us to consider the relation of reasoned assents to moral choices. We said, in Chapter 3, that the knowledge of surgery was not of itself fully perfective of the doctor unless this knowledge existed together with the decision to direct this practical knowledge to its recognized end of health. We said also that speculative knowledge—recall the just and unjust mathematician—was made fully perfective of man by moral choices that set up the existential conditions of the possession of speculative knowledge. Thus our own analysis would seem to demand that we consider the relation of taught knowledge to moral choices.

First off, we should say clearly what we said above, that knowledge is not the cause of choices in the sense that fire cooks an egg by making water boil. Since free choices cannot be so caused and remain free, there is no question that knowledge, or anything else for that matter, is such a cause. Whatever may be the relation of knowledge to choice, we can safely say it is not one of efficient causality, where knowledge efficiently causes moral choice.

This negative conclusion does not get us very far into our problem. We need to see positively the role that knowledge plays in choice and specifically the role of college-taught knowledge in good moral choices. We shall proceed, first, to consider the act of choice and the role of knowledge in such acts; next, to see what good moral choices are; and finally, to see what teaching does for good moral choices.

Choice is a kind of action or activity. In the most precise sense, choice is an internal decision to do something, say, pick up this book. The external action of picking up the book is more a consequence of choice than choice itself. At times we designate the external action as chosen, and this is correct. But physically picking up this book is a chosen action only because it was preceded by the internal decision to do so. The same holds for the freedom of actions. The external act is called free only because the internal act of choice was freely made. Choice, then, is properly the internal decision to do something, and only in a derived sense can the external act be called a choice.

If one is a thoroughgoing mechanist, he will explain human choice much as he explains the actions of parts of a machine or the action of chemical elements in forming a compound. His starting point will be the mechanical principle of opposite and equal reaction. Choice will then become a response to a stimulus, so that if stimulus X is given, response Y follows. In this view man acts the way he does because of conditioned reflexes that set up reaction patterns, all explained by chemico-electrical forces acting according to the laws of classical mechanics. Such an explanation of human choice gets blinded by the desire to share in the brilliant success of the physical sciences. But there are two facts, attested by common experience, that preclude a mechanical explanation. One is that a violent reaction may follow a slight stimulus, or a slight reaction follow a strong stimulus. Think of the man on a crowded bus who becomes violently angry when he is jostled a bit by the crowd. The second fact is that human actions are directed to a goal and purposive. There is no mechanical way of explaining either of these facts.

A second explanation is based on a biological pattern in which action has its source in man and is not merely a reaction to an outside source. The organic source of human action consists in drives—desires, feelings, emotions. Such drives are purposive and goal-seeking, provided one understands the purpose or goal as subjective; that is, the release of tension caused by the energy of the drive. The objects sought have little to do with the action other than to release the energy of the drive. In a sense, this drive theory of human action is not fully freed from mechanical overtones. If objects of desire are only triggers to release the built-up energy of the drive, the picture given is not too different from that of a stretched rubber band ready to go into action when a trigger releases it. And on this point the drive theory founders. It can be granted that there are some purely biological drives that show up in consciousness as emotional energy seeking release. But such drives are not specifically human and are not the central factors in choice. In choice the object is more than a trigger or release mechanism. Common experience testifies that our desire is for something and that we shrink from something. Choice consists in choosing this thing or action, rejecting that thing or action. To reduce the object's role in choice to that of a release mechanism is actually to render choice unintelligible.

The contemporary explanation introduces the factor of value or motivation to explain choice.[1] Both value and motive pertain to the object, though in different ways. A value is what is known as good and consequently is the possible object of desire. What I consider good I can also desire. What I consider bad from every viewpoint I cannot desire for myself; what I consider bad from one viewpoint but good from another I can desire insofar as it is good. The good is equated with what is known as able to be desired. Food, for example, is a material good and is a value for a hungry man. He can desire it if he so chooses. Of course, he can also refuse to choose it, say, because he is on a diet. If he chooses not to eat this food, the food does not cease to be a value for him. It is still desirable even though, for reasons other than hunger, he chooses not to eat it. He may also decide to eat this food, even against the prescription of his dietary program. In this last situation, the food is not only able to be desired and therefore a value; it is actually desired and becomes a motive.[2]

Motives are values that draw a man into actual choosing. In the example above, food for the man who kept his diet was a value and not a motive—his motive was the good of health; food for the man not following his diet was more than a value—it was also a motive. Notice that the food was a value for both men; it was a motive only for the one who decided to break his diet. Two facts are indicated in this uncomplicated example. One is that values are not enough to account for choices; only motives do that. The other, that values are common and objective, whereas motives are personal and subjective. We shall consider the second fact first.

If one confuses values with motives, one easily supposes that values are subjective and personal, just as motives are. But nothing grounds this supposition beyond the original confusion. For values that were subjective would not be values at all. Value is the known desirability of a thing. Knowledge is thus the condition of a thing's being known as valuable, but knowledge does not constitute the value of the thing. What constitutes value is the thing as good and insofar as it is good. The role of knowledge in relation to values is twofold. That of speculative knowledge is to report the good or valuable aspects of what is; that of practical knowledge is to direct action to make the good (valuable) thing exist. In either case value is in the thing (known or made), not in the subject. A test case would be one where knowledge was erroneous. Suppose that a lad, raised with thieves, thought that stealing was a sign of adult courage. Stealing would be a value for him. Is this not a subjective value, seeing that stealing in fact is not a good act? We could then say that stealing was a subjective value for him, but objectively it is the opposite of a value. As handy as this answer seems to be, it is no good. Stealing to him was as objective as anything can be. He looked on stealing as one definite way to be courageous. The good of stealing consisted in the action of stealing. This is a thing, the action of stealing, and that is what is valuable to him because it was an exercise of courage (for him). No doubt he is wrong in his estimate. But he is not wrong in thinking that values are objective. He thinks as everyone else does, that things or actions (in this case, stealing) are valuable.

In fact, if values were subjective, they could not be desirable. As subjective they would already modify the subject. And what you have you cannot desire or seek to possess. In order to be values, desirables, they must be objective. At this spot, one who thinks values are subjective will appeal to the knowledge condition of values. That is, things are and are good; they become values when known. Since knowledge is thought to be subjective, values also become subjective owing to their being in knowledge in order to be values. The mistake here is precisely parallel to that above. For knowledge can never be subjective. It must be objective at the price of not being knowledge if it is not. True, knowledge must be in a subject knowing, just as desire (of value) must be in a subject desiring. But the opposite is also true. Without an object known or a good desired, there is no knowledge or desire. Knowledge of no object, nothing, would not be knowledge and therefore not even subjective, just as the desire of nothing is not desire. Nor is erroneous knowledge such because it is only subjective. Error in knowledge arises from a mistaken objectivity, not from lack of objectivity. To say this paper is black is a false proposition. What makes it false is that it states to be objective what is not objective. If erroneous knowledge were subjective, it is hard to see how it could possibly be erroneous or even be knowledge.

Values are not subjective either on the score that they are known or on the score that they are good. From both aspects they necessarily are objective. But the same cannot be said of motives. These latter are factors in free choices. Motives, as values actually desired, draw a man into making free choices. And since free choices are self-originative and therefore personal and private, so also must motives be personal and private. In fact, man is free precisely because his motives as motives—that is, as actually desired values—are his own because he wants these motives to move him.

This last point needs further consideration.[3] Suppose our hungry dieter is faced with two goods or values. One is the food that he especially likes. The other value is the good of health, which demands here that he keep his weight down. Both goods are values. Now the time is come for him to decide what he will do, eat the food or refuse it. Notice that neither value of itself requires that he choose it and reject its alternative. Move the example one step forward. Suppose he takes sides; he chooses to eat the food. The value that is food is now a motive; it moved him to choose it. The value of health is only a value and not a motive since it did not move him. Ask this question: Did the motive, food, account for choice? The answer is yes. The reason he chooses to eat was the good of this food. But ask a further question: Does the food account for its being a motive rather than just a value? The answer has to be no. Otherwise choice would be impossible in our example. Recall, health was also a value. If a value becomes a motive because it is a value, health too would be a motive. Then food would move him actually to eating, and health would move him actually to refuse the food. Were such the case, choice would be impossible. But in the example a choice was made, as choices frequently are made in life. The facts, therefore, require us to say that although the food as motive accounts for his choice, the food does not account for its being a motive.

What accounts for a value's being a motive is the freedom of man. The dieter made the value, food, into a motive when he decided to be moved by the good or value of the food. Before that decision the food was a value. In the act of deciding the food became a motive. This making a value be a motive is the very core of the free act. If values were necessarily motives, man would not be free. If values were made into motives by some cause other than the person himself, he would not be free, as happens in compulsive neurotics. The free man is the one who determines his own motives. His free actions are those in which he converts a value into a motive by making it his own value here and now.

Motives, then, must be personal because they are constituted such by the originative and personal act of man. But values are not so constituted. Values are constituted by the goodness of objects. Only on this supposition can they become personalized motives, for there must be something objective to move a man to seek it. Motives that moved to nothing would not be motives. Thus values are objective as the necessary requisite of their becoming motives for the subject choosing. That is why man must decree value to objects, whether they are actually valuable or not, in order to have them move him; as the young thief in the example above had to see stealing as courageous act (even though it is not) in order to be moved to steal.

Some thinkers would deny that men are free if they are moved to act because of values which are objective. To them freedom consists essentially in the undetermined or undecided state of a man faced with possible choices. No doubt this state is impressive in human experience, and one who wanted to show that man is free before he acts would pitch on this data as the very quintessence of freedom. He ought to be consistent, however, and say that motives invade freedom because they move a man from being undecided to being decided. He ought also to say that free acts are undetermined acts, since freedom is indetermination and acts done under freedom ought to keep the quality of being free, the quality of indetermination. Since neither consequence fits the facts, it makes more sense to take another look at "indetermination freedom." Then we see that not being decided or determined to any one action is only a prior condition of freedom. When that condition is not present, as in machines, there is no possibility of freedom. But freedom, rather than its condition, is primarily the act in which we determine our own actions, self-determination. That, we said, consists in a man deciding what value will be his value, a motive for him. Thus free acts are not only determined acts; they are the most determined of all actions because self-determined.[4]

The free acts that interest us at present are those that are morally good choices. Such are choices that set the higher goods (values) as the ones that are motives for the one choosing. Perhaps the term "higher good" is not as precise as some would desire, but it has a place in common language and literature. A much better term would be "properly human good," meaning a good that animals do not seek and that men do, such as knowledge for its own sake, self-esteem, self-realization. Better still, "a good that is always good." This quality of being always good, always perfective of the one choosing, brings us directly to the field of morality and the moral good. Justice, for example, is always good for man in the same way honesty is, and injustice and dishonesty never perfect a man. But some goods are good at one time, at another not; some goods also are good for one person and not good for another. Think of food in relation to a starving man and a man who has just banqueted, or of candy for a growing child and a diabetic. Clearly, "good" is a term with many meanings.

There is no doubt that a human being first experiences the good as the pleasant. And since pleasure is a subjective reaction, our first experience of the good is in terms of its yield of pleasure, which is a subjective state. Not only is this our first experience of what is good, but the pleasure criterion remains operative throughout life, so that some things appear good solely because of the pleasure they yield. When such things, say, a favorite food, cease to produce pleasure they no longer appear to us as good in the same way. Thus goods, judged such by the pleasure criterion, are obviously variable for different persons and from time to time for the same person, because of the fact that the individual person and even circumstances of the same person constitute half of the relation of such goodness. The relativity of such goods does not arise from the mere fact that they do or do not cause pleasure in this or that setting. If we drop the norm of pleasure-producing and take that of suitability or need-answering, with or without pleasure—say, bitter medicine—the same relativity shows up because the good thing is still judged by the response of the individual subject. The person who is not sick has no need of medicine, bitter or sweet, and it therefore has no goodness as answering a need that does not exist. Any good, whether it is looked at as purely pleasurable or as purely satisfying a need, may thus appear as a relative good.[5]

Some goods, however, hold a special status in man's estimation. Instead of their answering to our demands, we find that we must answer to their demands. They are not good because of some relation they have to us; rather we are good because of our relation to them. Such things are honesty, justice, temperance, courage, kindness, prudence; also reverence, love, obedience to God. That these goods are expressed abstractly should not obscure the fact that they exist in concrete actions, as justice exists in the action of paying one's honest debts. The power of such actions to satisfy or give pleasure is of no great consequence. Their excellence is that they make men good, not that they make men satisfied or feel pleasant. No doubt the man who wants to be good will also feel satisfied, and at times pleased, with his just actions, just as the man who wants to keep his money may feel miserable after paying his honest debts because he no longer has the money he wants. But justice is not good because it satisfies; it satisfies, when it does, because it is good and good for man.

Moral goods, then, appear as always good because they are not relative to this or that man or to man at all. They are simply good. They can thus be called higher goods in the sense that they make a man good who takes them as motives. Choices that have these moral goods as the motive are morally good choices, made good by the moral good chosen. And morally good choices are what make a man morally good or virtuous. They also make him good without qualification or relativity, since moral goods are themselves not relative.

Our analysis of morally good choices puts us in position to see the role of knowledge in such choosing. First of all, knowledge makes us aware of the values of things. Value, we said, is a known good. Goods that are not known are neither values nor nonvalues; they simply are and are good. Goods that are known become values by standing in knowledge as goods. Merely to be in knowledge is not sufficient. A rhesus monkey, for instance, would see no economic value in a hundred dollar bill. The bill would stand in his knowledge, for he could see, touch, and smell it; but it would not be there as an economic good and consequently not be an economic value. It is important to recall that this insistence on value being a known good does not deny the objectivity of values. Things are; they are good and valuable in themselves, whether known or not. They become actual values, though, as opposed to being possible values, when they stand in the knowledge of one seeing their good. Still, it is the object that stands in knowledge, not the subject; it is the good of the object that stands in knowledge, not something proper to the subject.

Thus the first role of knowledge in choosing is to present values, to present things as good, as choosable. Knowledge, therefore, first of all supplies the objects of choice. But knowledge does more than this. Its second role is to grade goods as being more or less good. Among goods whose only good is the ability to yield pleasure, the criteria for more good is that of more pleasure produced. Goods that fulfill needs are seen to be as important as the need they fill. If the need is seen as more important than any possible pleasure, a good fulfilling a need will be rated higher than the good producing pleasure. At the top of the class of goods are the "higher goods," or moral goods. For knowledge presents these goods as what is always good and not merely as pleasant or as fulfilling a need. To such goods knowledge sees that man is bound by obligation. They make him good, as distinct from pleased or satisfied. The question at the moment is not what a man considers himself bound to. The point here is that whatever a man knows as what he is bound to is determined by his knowledge of it as the supreme good. And this grading of goods is the work of knowledge.

The first and second roles of knowledge, to supply objects of choice and to grade such objects, are prior to the act of choosing. Knowledge also plays a third role, this one in the act of choosing, the act of making a value become a motive. We said above that no value is necessarily a motive for man. He must make a value be his motive. Since choice cannot be blind and be human, choice must be made with the presence of knowledge. Here is the third role of knowledge, acting in concert with will: to know one value as best for the chooser here and now. Such knowledge is not merely the report that one value is higher than another. A report would be about a value as a value. Since no value has of itself what it takes to be a motive, no knowledge of value can by itself be a knowledge of a motive. Beyond knowledge is added the factor of the will, the desire that this value be a motive. With this factor present and directive of knowledge, knowledge then reports this value as best for the chooser here and now. Thus choice has knowing at its core, though a preferential knowing. The dieter chooses to eat the fattening food because he thinks this is best (his motive) for him here and now. He thinks this best for him here and now because he wants so to think.

Each role that knowledge plays in the act of choice is one of specification. The first role supplies possible objects (values) of choice. Since objects specify acts—an action is designated and distinguished by what it is action towards —supplying possible objects is a kind of remote specification. Grading values according to their objective excellence is also a kind of specifying, since it distinguishes and rates objects that may be chosen. But both supplying and grading values are only preparatory to full specification. In its last role knowledge fully and completely specifies the act of choice when it knows one value as best here and now, thereby making a value into a motive. The choice of the dieter to eat the fattening food is specified completely and finally by his knowledge that this value will be his motive. The act of choice is achieved, the decision to eat the fattening food.

Our interest in choice and the role of knowledge in choice is to see what college teaching has to do with good moral choices. We have, therefore, two limitations to our consideration. First, there is the kind of choices in question. They are such as deal with the higher goods or values. The second limitation is that arising from college teaching. We distinguished two aspects of learning from a teacher, the assents made and the existential conditions of such assents. It would seem, then, that our next step is to consider the two aspects of learning from a teacher in relation to each of the three roles of knowledge in choices of the higher values. This would give us six steps: assents relative to the three roles of knowledge and the existential conditions relative to the three roles of knowledge.

A second line of attack suggests itself. Since the first two roles of knowledge in choice are properly and only knowledge, it might be thought that reasoned assents supply values as objects and grade them, while the existential conditions pertain to the third role of knowledge, that of knowing a value as mine here and now. There is some truth to this distinction. Existential conditions are closer to actual choice than mere knowledge of what is of value or what the higher values are. The state of appetites, for instance, of the learner affects not only his learning but his choices too. Again, the virtuous actions of a living teacher, themselves the external result of morally good choices, are closer to actual choice because the values are concretized in existing actions. Still, the fact remains that even the presence of values existing in the concrete actions of a teacher is no guarantee that the student's choices will be good. What alone guarantees his good choices is his own personal, private decisions. This fact should not be blurred. And any plan of consideration that tends to blur it should be suspect from the beginning.

What I propose to do is this, to keep reasoned assents and their existential conditions as a unit, taught knowledge, and then to ask what this unit has to do with making the higher values motives of actual choice. Thus we shall limit our consideration of teaching to the first two roles of knowledge. The reason for this limitation is obvious from our analysis of free choice. The third role of knowledge is such that it follows preference in the actual choice and is therefore not a determiner of choice but is rather determined by choice; the chooser, that is, sees things this way because he wants them so seen. Such knowledge is made by choice and in no way makes choices. The knowledge that influences choice will have to be the knowledge that is prior to choice itself, knowledge in its first two roles. We shall consider these, but in reverse order. Here are our questions. What does taught knowledge do in relation to the higher values? What does taught knowledge do to keep values present at the moment of choice? If moral values, by teaching, can be made to appear as truly higher and present at the moment of choice, knowledge does as much as it, or anything else short of God, can do for moral choices.

Our first question deals with the teachability of values. Those who confuse values with motives must say that values cannot be taught; otherwise they would then be saying what is patently false, that motives can be taught. Those who distinguish values from motives, as we did, are not caught in this bind. That motives cannot be taught leaves untouched the teachability of values. To decide if values can be taught requires that values, as values and not motives, should be tested against the norm of the teachability of knowledge.

That norm, we concluded above, is that knowledge is teachable when it deals with facts that can be commonly possessed; or, in its negative statement, the more individual and private the facts are the less teachable they are. Motives, because they are personal and private in the fullest degree, are not teachable at all. Values, however, deal with the worth of things. Since things and their worth are objective, they are facts; thus values are facts about the worth of something. When value or worth is taken as pleasure-giving, such facts may or may not be common.

One may find chocolate candy pleasant; another may find it cloying. Again, if values are taken as suitable or answering a need, they may or may not be common facts, depending on whether the need is common or not. One may need much exercise in order to keep healthy; another may need relatively little. Need-answering values, therefore, are not fully teachable.[6] Some needs may be common to a group; for example, the need of special knowledge in order to become a lawyer. All who need the lawyer's knowledge because they intend to practice law can be taught the value of the knowledge necessary for a lawyer. Those who do not need to possess such knowledge themselves will not consider, nor can they be taught, that the lawyer's knowledge is valuable for them to know. The limited teachability of values read as "suitable to me" is owing to the relative factor always present in such values.

But this factor of relativity is not present in what we called the higher or moral values. The moral worth of any one thing or action is not due to its power to answer needs, even when it does. Its excellence is that it makes a man good. Moreover, it will make any man's action good, not just this or that man's. Moral values are thus common facts about the worth of things and actions; and, therefore, the knowledge of such facts is teachable. And notice that they are common as values; they are the goods that make every man good. Were moral goods only teachable as a good a man could take or leave to suit himself, they would be no more teachable than relative values are. But moral values do not stand as relative. They are proper to every man. Thus they are teachable precisely as values; they are values for every man in all circumstances; and as such they are teachable to every man.

Another way to say the same thing is to say that moral values are established by reason. Values whose formal goodness is as answering a need are established by the need and its presence in consciousness. Such needs are proper to the subject, and the values answering them gain from the person's preference. But moral values do not get their value from, nor are they justified by, personal preference. They must be established by reason. For they deal with what is beyond preference and is therefore based on some necessary relation of man to moral goods. Necessary relations are the province of reason. Considering what man is and what the moral values are, reason sees that a man who does not value these is to that extent failing to be a man. That is, reason sees that moral values are necessarily the good of any man. Reasons, open to all, can be given to prove that honesty and prudence and justice and charity perfect every man. Reasons can be given to prove that their opposites—dishonesty, imprudence, injustice, and cruelty—corrupt any man. The conclusion, open to all because provable by reason, is that moral values are necessarily the good for every man and are therefore always good for man.

This means, of course, that moral values are teachable as values. Student assents regarding moral values are made in all the morally related knowledges that a college teaches. These, we said in Chapter 5, are history, literature, political science, philosophy, and theology. Such knowledges receive special emphasis in Catholic colleges. Among them philosophy and theology, both speculative and moral, hold primacy because of their special relation to the knowledge and ordering of values. Speculative philosophy, as we said in Chapter 5, helps the student understand why good choices make a man good; just as speculative theology helps a student understand how the choice of a limited good, say, to speak the truth in this situation, is implicitly the choice of the unlimited good, God Himself. And both philosophy and theology have branches that deal explicitly with the higher values that should become motives for good choices.

Since our question concerns teaching and the higher values, we may as well go immediately to theology as the foremost knowledge establishing values. When we considered the faith and theology in Chapter 5, we limited ourselves to the role of faith as setting the existential conditions of learned assents in other fields of knowledge. Hence in that framework it was not necessary to distinguish between faith and theology. Here we shall consider faith as reasoned assents—that is, as theology—since we are asking how the faith establishes the excellence of the higher values.

Reason presents God as the cause of the world and all in it because He is being itself. As being, He is good and the cause of all good, and therefore supreme in value and the cause of all value. True as such assents are, they are far from the rich truth that theology presents. For theology shows that God is also the Father as well as cause, a Father who creates according to His Son (His Wisdom) because of His Love (the Holy Spirit). As personal God, He creates out of love as persons do, so that creation is now a gift, the language of love. The fatherhood of God, then, is seen to be the infinite prototype of the finite fatherhood of man, making the latter appear in its full goodness and value by giving the full ground or reason for its value. The fatherhood of man, when he is a father, is a crowning moral value because God is father. So also for all the eminent values, such as acts of honesty, justice, and prudence, on both the natural and supernatural level. These are supreme goods for man because they are what God is, who is good itself. No firmer guarantee can be found for the excellence of any value than that it is what God is. And the student making such theological assents never needs to change his conclusion either that these goods are higher or why they are higher.

Take a second area of theological knowledge, that about man. If, as E. Schrödinger said,[7] the purpose of the natural sciences as well as of all purely human knowledge is to know what man is, theology must rank above all such knowledges, since it tells us more about man; namely, that he was created by God to His own image and likeness, and given special help to achieve full union with God; that man, in the persons of Adam and Eve, refused to obey God—to image God in their actions—and was deprived of these special helps so that man no longer could achieve what he was created for; that the Father, out of infinite love, sent His Son to become a man in order to redeem and guide man back to the Father with the special help of the Holy Spirit; that man is now able, through the sacraments and the sacrifice of Christ, to achieve his appointed end, personal union with the triune God. These tremendous assents of theology give men a whole new vision of human values because they give a new and true knowledge of the end of man. And the end of man is the value of values for man, the one value that gives goodness and value to all lesser values.

This last point can be seen in any specific way of considering the end of man. Take that of self-development, one that we considered briefly in Chapter 5. It makes sense to say that man should—this *should* is the sign you are talking of the end of man—develop his powers and capabilities to the full. How does man do this? Certainly by developing his powers of thought, so he thinks well, and by developing his will, so he chooses well. So conceived, the perfection of man is properly called "self-development," for self is the central factor. Man seeks to gain values for self; he acts so as to develop self; the result is acquiring something for self. The whole drift of this view is that perfection for man consists in appropriating, by knowledge and choice, as much as he can for self. Underneath this view there seems to be a massive selfishness, much like the hidden base of an iceberg.

Into this understanding of the perfection of man introduce the fact of the Incarnation, God made man. Here in a concrete example is what God thinks man should be. First of all, Christ seeks nothing for Himself; all is for the Father. He speaks what the Father sent Him to speak; He does what the Father sent Him to do; He saves those the Father sent Him to save. In the end, following the will of His Father, He gives His life for others, to bring them to the Father. And lest men miss this massive unselfishness of His, He put His wisdom in those unforgettable words, "For he who would save his life will lose it" (Math. 16:25). With this revealed truth ringing in our ears, we begin to see that the end of man is not something purely human— a perfectly developed man—but something also divine. That is, a man must leave himself, go out of himself,[8] in a sense give himself up because what will perfect him is beyond his nature and the powers of his nature. He must be perfect as His heavenly Father is perfect, a thing he can do only by throwing himself on the goodness of God. Self-development is still the end of man. Only now it means using mind and will well, not as what brings perfection to man but as what will lead man out of himself to God.

Notice what the theological knowledge of man does for human values. The dignity of men is infinitely enhanced because they are now potentially divine, potentially the sons of God and destined to be at home with their Father in heaven. The mind of man gains the inviolable right to the facts, for in these the human mind must discover the God who will answer the thirst of his mind for what is. The will of man gains its inviolable right to freedom because the only way man can go out beyond himself to what perfects him is by his free decisions to commit himself to the goods of God and through them to God Himself. Even man's body gains in value. One day his body will live in the presence of God, just as the human body of Christ does today. Nothing about man remains purely human. Everything human is destined to share in the divine. Thus it is not fully correct to say that theology establishes human values as human. Rather, theology establishes human values by converting them into values more than human.

In order to show that taught knowledge, especially theology, establishes the higher values by giving a reason for their supremacy, we have considered one specific good, fatherhood, and one general good, the end of man. More examples would only be repetitious, seeing that the end of man sets the purpose of life and this in turn gives sense and dignity to every value short of that end. Only one other point should be added to indicate the teachableness of theological knowledge. Abstract knowledge is highly teachable in itself, but when it comes to actual learning from a teacher abstractions are seldom enough. That is why teachers find it necessary to appeal to examples and diagrams and models, for these latter are concrete and imaginative presentations that help the mind to rise to the abstract truth behind and beyond the examples. Theology considered precisely as teachable is singularly blessed in having a perfect example to appeal to. The known life of Christ, with its wealth of circumstance, action, and explanation, supplies not only a living model, not only a lovable model, but also a perfect model, in which what is, is also what should be. To see what the higher values are and why they are higher, one need only turn to the life of Christ to see them exemplified in concrete known choices.

Our argument runs this way. Choices cannot be taught because motives cannot be taught. But motives, first of all, must be values, known goods. Values, as objective, are teachable when they are common. The higher values are teachable because they are common and therefore can be established by reason to be values for all men at all times. Thus the higher values can be taught as having the steady right to become motives of actual choice. The ground for the higher values is seen to be human nature itself. Then faith as theology steps in to teach the higher values as being more than human, as being grounded ultimately in the divine goodness of God. How much more do moral values, seen now in the light of theology, have the right to become the motives of choice! Teaching has done part of its work well by establishing the full excellence of the moral good.

The other part of teaching's work—our second question— is to aid in keeping moral values present to consciousness at the moment when choices are to be made. First of all, taught values that are reasoned assents share in the stability of reason itself. The other possible source of judging values is emotions or feelings, which are notoriously unstable left to themselves. The ground for this instability is the sort of values that emotions respond to. The pleasant and the needful are what bring emotions into play. Since pleasure depends partly on the state or condition of the individual, the pleasant varies, and so must the emotions. The same is true of the needful. Hence emotions are variable and dependent on the accidents of individual circumstances. Reason, however, is not limited to the pleasant or the needful. Because it knows the good whether it is pleasant or needful or neither, it is not bound to variable circumstances. It can reason to the good that is always good, the necessary good for man. Values established by reason are seen to be stable values, made stable by the reasons given for them.

This is true of all reasoned assents, whether based on experience or on revelation; but it is especially true of the latter. For revelation, as we said above, humanizes reason. That is, it brings the moral values established by reason into a more personal and humanly significant framework. The God reason can prove is not nearly so significant to man as the Father of revelation. The creaturehood of man has none of the human warmth of the sonship of man; just as submission to God—the moral law—is rather cold compared with the dependence of the child upon his Father in heaven. What reason relying on experience shows as true, reason relying on revelation shows as thoroughly human and attractive. In this way emotion is brought to the side of reason, increasing the stability that is properly reason's birthright, increasing also the chances that such values will be present at the moment of choice.

There is a third character of reasoned assents that needs to be considered here. Taught assents are caught up in a train of thought that goes from data to principle to conclusion, in which each step has been made clear to the student. The presence in consciousness of any one of these factors in the line of thought will tend to bring back the whole train. And where assent is reasoned from revealed as well as natural data, the original factors are increased. The starting point is not only what one learns from personal experience; it can also be the word of God. Either beginning point can ground such reasoned assent. Thus with a double set of data and two lines of reasoning the likelihood of recall is doubled. A person, for example, faced with the extreme need of another man can see his helping action both as what is fitting and what is Christlike. Either line of thought or both can make the value of charity present at the moment of choice. Again, a college student tempted to cheat in an examination can see the evil of such action as an act against his rational and social nature; he can also see the action as being against the precept of Christ. Either or both lines of thought can make honesty as a value present to the mind.

Our last example, of cheating, introduces what is sometimes called a negative value. But this designation is a misnomer for a choice between values, one absolute and the other relative. The two values that enter a decision to cheat are these: good grades and honesty. Since both cannot be had—at least the cheater supposes this—to choose the better grades is to give up honesty, a good that is always good, in order to gain the relative good of good grades. Thus evil choices consist in preferring lesser and relative goods to higher and absolute goods. And the knowledge of what the higher goods are and how the lesser goods should be related to them is essential to good choices. When this knowledge becomes a settled view it constitutes a man's understanding of life. It can also be called a life ideal that stands as the constant and ever-present matrix from which all choices arise and the constant norm to which all choices must answer.[9]

A life ideal is a complex value that holds all particular values in an ordered unity, giving each its proper place and weight. Pleasure is accorded its place; relative values are seen as temporal and circumstantial, absolute values as essential and timeless. Such ordering of values is possible only where reason performs its work well, since only reason is able to decipher the relation of value to needs, of needs to the nature of man, and of the nature of man to what perfects it. Lesser values, ordered by reason, thus gain in stature by being given a place in a unity dominated by moral values, so that even lesser values share in the moral excellence of the whole complex value. At the same time moral values gain the great boon of being supported and strengthened, rather than opposed and weakened, by pleasurable and suitable goods. This hierarchical unity of values is sometimes called a philosophy of life, for it is a man's understanding of himself in terms of what is important to him or in terms of the norms against which he judges himself. But whatever name is given to this complex value it serves to direct and unify the choices and actions of life.

It is also consistently present to consciousness, one condition of its being operative on choices. All choices must be made in the light of this life ideal, even those not according to it. The man, for example, who considers telling the truth an essential good in his life ideal may possibly lie on this or that occasion. But he does not do so without being conscious of his failure, for his life ideal is part and parcel of his knowledge of himself. It continues, therefore, to be present to him until he changes the pattern of this ideal. Nor is the change easy, if his ideal was the result of a serious, sustained use of reason. Reason can be overcome by sudden passion, but it cannot be silenced completely until it has been blinded by repeated passion and reduced to a mere tool of desire.

Granted the importance for choices of a well-reasoned life ideal, one must also grant the importance of Catholic college teaching for moral choices. Not only the knowledge learned but the conditions of learning unite to articulate and illumine a life ideal worthy of the Christian man. What reason discovers about nature and man and God by artistic and scientific knowledge is also seen as reinforced and completed by an equally scientific knowledge of what God has told man. Both knowledges, developed and perfected together, come together as the firm, interlocking grounds for a life ideal that unifies the values of both time and eternity. What, beyond the family and the Church, can do as much as teaching does to build up a Christian life ideal? What more can anyone or anything human do to insure the good moral choices of another?

CHAPTER 8

SUMMARY

By way of summary we shall try now to formulate an answer to the question that gave rise to this book. Our question was stated in two ways. In the first chapter, the question was put in terms of teaching and virtue in a

Catholic liberal arts college. In Chapter 2, the question was put in terms of the objectives of a liberal arts college. These are not two questions; they are two formulations of the same question. However, we shall treat them as two and formulate an answer to each separately, since the double formulation may add at least the clarity of repetition.

Our first question was: What does a Catholic liberal arts college, in its teaching, do for the moral virtue of the student? Recall the sense of the question. It arose from the twofold realization that colleges profess above all to teach and that moral virtues above all cannot be taught. There would be no problem if a college could simply ignore the moral virtue of its students. But no human institution proposing to perfect the young could possibly defend this position. Here, then, is the ground of our problem. Colleges, as institutions perfective of the young, must be concerned with the moral virtue of their students. Colleges must also, in order to be liberal arts colleges, be concerned with teaching the arts and sciences.

This double concern could result in two sets of actions, one ordered to learning, another to developing moral virtue. The arguments against this solution are two. First it supposes that extracurricular activities directly produce virtue—just as teaching directly produces knowledge—a supposition that stands in need of proof, seeing that virtue resides in free choices. Second, if moral virtue is put on a par with knowledge, it will not stay there, since it always has the right to take precedence as long as education is considered fully perfective of the young. Let virtue take precedence over knowledge, and the liberal arts college becomes suspect.[1] Since the separation of the two, knowledge and virtue, seems to lead nowhere, we asked our question so as to keep the two together. That is, what does a college in its teaching do for good moral choices?

Our question thus focused on teaching and consequently on knowledge. Consideration of knowledge made it clear that there is a difference, though no opposition, between the knowledge known and the state of its possession. Both practical and speculative knowledge must exist in some existential setting. And this setting or state of possession, more determined by choice than by assent, is the ultimate reason why knowledge, besides being the perfection of the man as knower, is also perfective of man as man. The social function of the college would demand that the knowledge taught be perfective of man as man. Hence, the necessary interest of the college in both the knowledge taught and its state of possession.

This consideration of the two factors of knowledge opened up a different approach to teaching. Teaching can be looked at as something proper to the teacher or as something in the student being taught. Both views are possible because teaching is a transient action, one that begins in one being (the teacher) and ends in another (the student). A metaphysician would say that the transient action of the agent is in the patient. Common sense would say that the wood, not the carpenter, gets made into a bench. Thus the causative action of the carpenter exists more, and therefore more clearly, in the bench than in the carpenter. The same holds for teaching. The student's taught assents are the culmination of teaching, teaching in its most complete and final stage. Thus if one wishes to consider teaching where it is most teaching, he will consider the assents made by the student with the help of the teacher. This view of teaching makes it possible to give the proper attention to both the assents made and the conditions under which such assents are possessed by the student.

In order to be more precise about the kinds of assents made by college students we considered the various levels of assents made, those of spontaneous reasoning, of elaborated reasoning (whether artistic or reflective), and scientific assents. The liberal arts college concerns itself with assents of elaborated reasoning and especially and ideally with scientific assents, as the most teachable knowledge. The reason why such assents are most teachable is that the facts or objects dealt with can be common to all minds and therefore can be possessed by teacher and student alike. Where assents deal with facts that are not common and therefore not equally open to any mind, they are to that extent not teachable. Scientific assents are at every stage open to any properly trained mind. The elements in such assents are data, principles grounded in these data, and conclusions that follow from these principles applied to these data. In each step the object controls and justifies thought. If any factor not from the object enters the thinking process, the reasoning collapses and assent is not justified. What alone justifies scientific assent is the object considered, an object in principle open to any mind.

It is important to see that nothing whatever can cut into the line from data to assents concerning these data. It is just as important to see that assents about data must exist in a mind; in teaching, they must exist in the mind of the teacher first and then in the mind of the student. Thus other factors present in the mind of either teacher or student set up the existential conditions of the assents made through teaching. Sometimes a moral choice stands as the existential concomitant of a knowledge possessed; think of the surgeon who has decided to use his surgical knowledge in order to kill. Sometimes one kind of assent stands as the existential concomitant of another kind; think of the faith as present to a mind knowing philosophy. In neither situation does the existential concomitant, whether choice or other knowledge, make or unmake the assent or change it insofar as it is a correct assent. Choices and other knowledges modify the assenter, and only by affecting him can they have anything to do with his new assents.

It might seem that what only affects the learner, not his assents, is of little significance in teaching. Such is not the case. For the only thing besides the object that can affect assents is what affects the learner. Learning has two factors: the assent and the one assenting. Since the assent, if properly made, is fully controlled by the object and by nothing else, the only other legitimate way to influence an assent is through the learner. Now, grant that assents perfect the mind but not necessarily the man; grant secondly that colleges as human institutions ought to be interested in assents as perfective of the man and not merely of his mind; grant thirdly that the only avenue open to making assents perfective of the man is the existential posture of the learner and therefore of his assents; then one must conclude that a college ought, in the name of the reasoned assents it proposes to teach, to be concerned with the existential conditions of these assents.

In considering the existential concomitants of reasoned assents we limited our discussion to those that have some significance for moral virtue, especially those operative in a Catholic college. Some, we found, had their origin in the student himself, some in the teacher, and some in the faith common to both student and teacher. Those in the student derived from his moral habits, from the state of his emotions, and from the operation of his sense faculties. Those arising from the teacher and his teaching fell into two groups. First, his presentation of the subject matter, including such variables as selection of pertinent data, the emphasis and examples used, and relations to other knowledges and parenthetical comments; second, the concrete example of his own intellectual life, which gains respect from the student in proportion to what the student learns from him, thus becoming an ideal for student imitation—or its opposite.

The third source of existential determinants, the faith, present to both student and teacher, was seen as most operative because most pervasive. At times the faith puts one in the position to see where he made too hasty an assent in the arts or sciences. At times the faith supplies insights that make the work of reason striving for assent easier than if the faith had not been present. In the vital area of morally related knowledges, the faith can both lead reason by supplying facts (of revelation) not open to reason except as possibilities and strengthen reason by emphasizing a factor of the data easily obscured by human emotions. Finally, the faith humanizes the assents of reason, keeping them closer to God by giving each a role to play in the human task of finding God through knowledge and choice.

Actual learning from a teacher thus contains, besides the assents made, the existential conditions under which the assent is made. Both factors are important. When one factor—say, the existential conditions—is neglected, scientific assents tend to partial skepticism. Moreover, emphasis on scientific assents easily debilitates the springs of action and leaves the mind subject to unexamined existential conditions that are not the less operative because not recognized. When the existential conditions receive emphasis at the expense of scientific assents, the result is some form of anti-intellectualism, either one that thinks good will can supply for knowledge or that faith can supply for reason. In actual teaching what is needed is a balance between the two factors. The proper role of both assents and their existential conditions must be recognized and given attention. If not, prejudgments, not based on facts, will do the work of the factor not allowed its proper influence in the act of learning.

What has been said so far applies to all assents made in college. But some are of special significance for moral virtue because they are assents about the higher values. These can be taught because they deal with common facts, the same for all. The higher values can be seen to be absolute for all men in all circumstances. Here faith and reason coincide in making the same assent—one on experiential facts, the other on the word of God. Thus each gains from the other; the assents of reason gain added certainty from faith; the assents of faith gain added clarity from reason.

Since assents are knowledge, and not choice, one final point must be seen. Even assents about values are not motives until they enter choice. And no one can make a value be a motive except the person choosing, in the act of choice. Thus no teacher can teach choices. But he can teach what values are and which are absolute. College teaching does this. It also presents higher values in a way most likely to be present when the time comes for choices. The higher values are seen as absolute and therefore always valid and compelling. They are seen in two lines of reasoning, one from experience and one from faith, so that there is a double possibility of recall. They are seen finally as part of a unified value, a life ideal. Not only the assents about the higher values but all assents are brought into this life ideal through their existential conditions set up by the teacher's act of teaching and the faith in both teacher and student. All choices must be made in accord with, or at least consciously against, this unified life ideal.

Now we can answer our question about what the teaching in a Catholic liberal arts college does for moral virtue in the student. It teaches him assents in the arts and sciences in such a way that they can become part of a life ideal worthy of a Christian. The "can become" does not mean remote possibility. And every true assent can in this sense become part of such an ideal. The assents taught in a Catholic college are actually ordered by their existential conditions to be part of a Christian ideal of life. This character of being so ordered resides in the assents themselves; it is they that are ordered. But we still must say only that they can become, for accepting a life ideal or deciding to act according to its demands involves free choice as well as knowledge. Thus from the student's viewpoint his assents may or may not constitute the ideal according to which he in fact chooses; from the viewpoint of the assents and their ordering, they actually serve to constitute such an ideal. This point can be seen in a non-Catholic student in a Catholic college. The assents he makes by being taught are no less ordered to the same ideal than similar assents made by Catholic students. The only difference is that he may not fully comprehend the ordering, since he does not grasp its term, which is the end of man as seen by faith. But at the moment he should decide to embrace the faith, he would find that none of his assents learned in college need be changed. They always were, and are now seen to be, ordered by their existential conditions to this Christian ideal. This, then, is what a Catholic college does for the morality of the students: it teaches assents in themselves ordered to a definite Christian life ideal.

Notice that this answer respects fully the facts of teaching and of moral choice. The first fact is that moral virtue cannot be taught. Our analysis of teaching and the teachable indicated what could be taught and what could not be taught and why. Moral virtue was seen to be unteachable because of the factor of free choice essential to such actions. Thus we saved ourselves the fruitless effort of trying to find some way in which it could be taught.

At the same time we closed off another line of thought that is born of desperation. The line is this, that if teaching cannot cause virtue, then some other kind of action must. The fact is that only free choices of the individual cause virtue. Thus in the name of moral virtue there is no need to concoct nonteaching activities; and if one does, he should realize that their justification will have to be something else than their virtue-causing power. There are not two sets of activities in a college, one set causing knowledge and one causing moral virtue. This sort of dichotomy solves nothing; as a matter of fact, it only obscures two important facts about morality.

The first of these facts is that morality always suffers where there is no unity between moral choices and one's major occupation. Everyone is familiar with the caricature of the businessman who is moral on Sunday but carries on his weekday business with no reference to moral principles. Behind this caricature and making it possible is the truth that morality should pervade all one's actions. By the same token, all one's actions should promote morality. This means that any dichotomy between one's lifework and his morality will weaken both. Applied to the student, whose life is one of learning, any dichotomy between his making assents and his virtue will weaken both. His learning should be reinforced by virtue and be the learning of a virtuous man; his virtue should be that of a knowing person and should be reinforced by his acts of learning. If such is not the case, neither the knowledge nor the virtue of a student will be as perfective as either should be.

The second fact about morality—by far the more important for our present problem—is that free choices are made under knowledge. To choose requires that there be something to choose. This "something" is supplied by knowledge. Not that knowledge determines choices; in that case choice would not be free. But knowledge must specify what is chosen, or otherwise choosing would have no object and thus be impossible. Knowledge therefore holds a privileged place in choices, and good knowledge a privileged place in good choices. By good knowledge I mean both knowledge that is good as knowledge—that is, true— and knowledge that is knowledge of the good. The two are not opposed. Knowledge of the good is also true; if it is not true, it is not knowledge of the good. Now grant that man is drawn into choice by the known goodness of the things he finds around him. Grant also that things are seen to be good by knowledge of them and their goodness. Then true knowledge of the good is the specifying cause of good choices. Beyond the good knowledge all that is required for a good choice is the good will of the person to commit himself to what he knows is good.

An example will show what I mean. Suppose a student thinks that God is the cause of the evil in the world. He has grounds for disliking God, and his choice to reject the law of God as the norm of his action has a show of reason about it. Suppose he discovers the error in his thought; that is, he sees that God is the cause of all good, including the good of his own being, and is not the cause of evil. Should he still prefer to ignore the law of God, he can do so with no show of reason. He must do one of two things, either refuse to let this truth enter his consciousness at the moment of choice (he will think about God some other time) or get busy and construct out of whole cloth an opposed "truth" that will give the illusion of reasonableness to his bad choices. Either line of procedure shows the same point, that good knowledge is the normal, reasonable ground of good choices, and nothing else is.

Hence our answer to the question of teaching and morality fits the most essential fact about good choices. The normal ground of good choices is good assents. By teaching good assents in the proper existential conditions the liberal arts teacher does as much for the student's moral choices as can be done by anyone other than God and parents. True conclusions about the physical world, about man, and about God are the normal and reasonable ground for man's choosing freely to love and serve God—morality as a Christian understands it.

We turn now to the second statement of our question. This time we spoke of the objectives of a Catholic liberal arts college. In its most general form the question was: Is the objective of the Catholic liberal arts college virtue or knowledge or both? The general answer is that the objective is neither knowledge exclusively nor virtue exclusively but both. The difficulty is not in knowing if it is the correct answer; the difficulty is to see what one has said when he gives this answer. That is, how are knowledge and virtue related so as to be one objective of a college?

We tried out a number of relations proposed as clarifications of our question. One is that knowledge is the direct objective and virtue the indirect. Another is that both are equally direct objectives of the college. A third made knowledge the objective of the work (teaching) and virtue the objective of the worker (teacher). A fourth considered knowledge as the primary and virtue as the secondary objective. Each of these distinctions exhibits the same weakness, the tendency to dichotomize. Instead of joining the two in one objective they tend to separate and consequently must achieve unity by subordinating knowledge to virtue or virtue to knowledge. Both knowledge and virtue can hold superiority, but neither can stand subordination, not in a college.

The union of knowledge and virtue into one objective is not always a problem, even though one is not the other. Moral assents, the knowledge of absolute values, are so connatural to good choices that they tend to exist together. Thus there is no question of subordination here. Nor is there any great clarity added by saying, for instance, that the direct effect of some teaching in college is moral assents. As true as this is, it does not follow that virtue is the indirect effect of teaching moral assents. Knowledge is not the efficient cause of virtue, either directly or indirectly. Knowledge is only the connatural specifier of virtuous acts. But this is sufficient to give unity to the objective of teaching moral assents. Virtue is not subordinated to knowledge or knowledge to virtue.

The problem of the unity of the college's objective becomes more complicated when we turn to assents that are not about absolute values. Those, by supposition, are not possible specifiers of good choices. They deal with the true, not with the good; and the true is known, not chosen. In order to bring some unity into the objective of all college teaching, we introduced the distinction between assents made and the existential conditions of these assents. This distinction indicates a difference but not one that separates by dichotomizing. Thus assents about the true, because of their existential conditions set up by the teacher and by the faith of both teacher and student, become part of one understanding. Assents about the true exist in minds related to the good and therefore share in this relation. They become thereby unified with assents about the good. This one understanding then stands as a life ideal, the connatural specifier of good choices.

What, then, is the objective of a Catholic liberal arts college? The objective is knowledge of the arts and sciences as constituting a life ideal worthy of a Christian. The objective is not knowledge simply or moral virtue simply. It is both. Neither is primary, neither secondary. Knowledge of the arts and sciences must be present. It exists as the knowledge of a Christian soul. Both the knowledge and its existential conditions are primary and constitutive of the objective. Without either knowledge or its existential conditions a school will either not be a liberal arts college or it will not be Christian.

We can now, by using this objective, define a Christian liberal arts college. It is a community of those who love God seeking truth in the arts and sciences within their love of God. The changes in wording are obvious enough.

"Knowledge" is shifted to "seeking the truth" because a college is constituted by those who wish to make assents in the arts and sciences. "A life ideal worthy of a Christian" is shifted to "love of God" on the basis of Christ's words that "if you love me you will keep my commandments" (John 14:15). That truth is sought within the love of God indicates the faith as the main existential condition of all assents to the truth.

This definition has the advantage of showing clearly why the Church insists on having Christian liberal arts colleges. This insistence is sometimes misunderstood, as if it were a sign of the Church's perverse desire to take over wherever it can. It is argued that knowledge of the arts and sciences is a human concern, not a divine one. The Church has no commission, some think, to do other than preach the Word of God and save souls. It has the commission to educate for the next world—a sufficiently demanding task—and should leave education for this world in hands better able to do it. The Church's answer is that the arts and sciences are not fully human unless they are meshed with the faith. The point is not that the arts and sciences are not human or that they are not good in themselves; they are not good enough for a Christian unless they are arts and sciences within his love of God. And this existential factor, "within his love of God," is no inconsequential circumstance. It is constantly operative on the mind making assents in the arts and sciences, ordering them to something higher than themselves and thereby making them fully human. Such arts and sciences not only save minds; they also share in saving souls.

This position of the Church on liberal arts colleges also makes clear why there is no real substitute for a Catholic college. The financial burden of private schools will always impel men to find substitutes that are less burdensome. One possible substitute for Catholic liberal arts colleges will be religious foundations at public institutions. The rationale of such a plan is that Christian students will keep their faith in a public college, if theological knowledge, supplied by the private foundation, is taught them. I see no reason why this is not true. What is not true is the supposition behind the plan; namely, that the only interest of the Church in college education is that the students do not lose their faith. This is an interest, to be sure. But the Church has more interest in the human mind than that. Man can see God and see Him in everything, since He is there. Man can love God and love Him in everything, because He is in everything. Learning the arts and sciences as neutral towards God effectively separates them from a Christian's life. To add theology to such knowledge may well help save the student's soul. It will do nothing for the arts and sciences learned as neutral to theology. The result of such an education is not a Christian mind but a mind four-fifths neutral to God and one-fifth committed.

The Church has too much respect for the human mind to consider this an adequate substitute for a Catholic college. Not only the soul can be saved; the mind can also be saved. It will be saved by making it wholly Christian, not part Christian and part something else. Hence the Church says that those who wish to develop their minds by the arts and sciences should see that this development is thoroughly Christian. Such is done only in colleges where all assents are made within one's love of God.

CHAPTER 1

1 H. I. Marrou, *A History of Education in Antiquity*, trans. G. Lamb (London: Sheed and Ward, 1956), p. 90.
2 *Ibid.*, p. 285.
3 H. O. Taylor, *The Medieval Mind* (4th ed.; London: Macmillan Company, 1938), II, 435, 318, 330-31.
4 See Huston Smith, *The Purposes of Higher Education* (New York: Harper and Bros., 1955), especially pp. 37, 41, 43, 129, 132, 187.

CHAPTER 2

1 "The Catholic higher learning, then, has as its end learning and higher learning and Catholic higher learning. Any other end, no matter how excellent, is secondary, remote, and auxiliary" (Leo R. Ward, C.S.C., *Blueprint for a Catholic University* [St. Louis: B. Herder Book Company, 1949], p. 103). There are many prudential reasons for the position taken by Father Ward. And if I had to take sides today on the question proposed in his terms, I would go along with him. What I find inadequate in his position is his understanding of the problem.

2 *Education at the Crossroads* (New Haven: Yale University Press, 1943), p. 23. Another example can be seen in Neil G. McCluskey, S.J., *Catholic Viewpoint on Education* (New York: Hanover House, 1959). On page 75 he says that the school as such exists primarily "to develop the morally intelligent person." On page 77, where there is question of teaching so as to promote virtue, he says that "this secondary aim must remain incidental and subordinate to the primary activity of teaching."

3 *Education at the Crossroads*, p. 28.

4 Proper end means the same as direct end. We said above that directness, which is first used of local motion, can be applied to the intelligible similarity existing among an agent, its action, and the end achieved by action. Our example—a singer sings a song. This same data of similarity can be read in terms of what should be. A song ought to be produced by singing, and singing ought to be the action of a singer. Hence it belongs to, is proper to, a singer to produce a song by singing. A song is therefore the proper end of singing, one that belongs to it, the *proprium* of singing. All direct ends are proper ends, and all proper ends are direct ends. I shift in the text to "proper end" because the position I am considering here uses "proper end."

5 This position is defended by Kevin J. O'Brien, *The Proximate Aim of Education* (Milwaukee: Bruce Publishing Company, 1958). Father O'Brien takes his position from the words of Pius XI in his encyclical *Christian Education of Youth.*

6 See Ward, *Blueprint for a Catholic University*, p. 92.

7 Father O'Brien (*The Proximate Aim of Education*, p. 223) finds that novitiates differ from schools only because in the novitiates the perfection sought is that of the counsels. Perhaps the next question should be: How do the novitiates of religious communities differ from their juniorates or philosophates or theologates?

8 Eugene M. Burke, C.S.P., says: "But I am also sure that the primary purpose of Catholic education is one with the primary purpose of the Church of Christ—the salvation of souls" ("The Content and Methodology of the College Religion Program," *The Philosophy of Catholic*

Higher Education, ed. Roy J. Deferrari [Washington: Catholic University of America Press, 1948], p. 163).

9 "Matrimonii finis primarius est procreatio et educatio prolis; secundarius mutuum adjutorium et remedium concupiscentiae" (*Codex Juris Canonici*, Can. 1013, par. 1). Instead of using two secondary ends —the distinction would not help us here—I have used in the text one secondary end which includes the two of canon law.

10 See B. H. Merkelbach, O.P., *Summa Theologiae Moralis* (9th ed.; Paris: Desclée, 1954), III, 758-59, or F. M. Capello, S.J., *Tractatus Canonico-Moralis de Sacramentis* (6th ed.; Rome: Marietti, 1950), V, 9. Both authors insist that the secondary end is necessary and essential. Their very insistence indicates their concern lest the secondary end of marriage become strictly secondary.

11 Robert J. Henle, S.J., "Objectives of the Catholic Liberal Arts College," *Proceedings of Workshop on the Role of Philosophy and Theology as Academic Disciplines and Their Integration with Moral, Religious, and Spiritual Life of the Jesuit College Student* (New York: Jesuit Educational Association, 1962), V, 51.

CHAPTER 3

1 Maritain makes a similar distinction in his *Essay on Christian Philosophy* (trans. E. H. Flannery [New York: Philosophical Library, 1955] pp. 11, 12): "This means that we must distinguish between the *nature* of philosophy, or what it is in itself, and the *state* in which it exists in real fact, historically, in the human subject, and which pertains to its concrete conditions of existence and exercise." (Italics are his.)

2 This description is taken from Gerard Smith, S.J., *Natural Theology* (New York: Macmillan Company, 1951), pp. 1-6.

3 Some practical knowledge does guarantee its own good use; for example, prudence and in general the moral virtues. The reason is that such practical knowledge is an ordering of knowledge to the good; and since the good is one factor of action, such ordering includes its relation to action. This point can be seen in a negative example. The grammarian who deliberately breaks a law of grammar is a better grammarian than one who does so indeliberately. But the prudent man who is deliberately imprudent destroys his prudence and is therefore a worse man than the prudent man who is indeliberately imprudent, since an honest mistake does not make him imprudent.

4 Keep this example strictly in the field of mathematical knowledge. If one raises the question of the effect of other knowledge, which may be present to a mind, on mathematical knowledge, the position given in the text is not adequate.

5 Speculative knowledge, as considered in the text is knowledge in this life. In the beatific vision speculative knowledge will perfect man completely. Speculative knowledge in this life is abstractive and therefore partial, always leaving a gap between the knower and full reality. Love, however, can bridge this gap because love terminates in the full existent. Thus man, in order to perfect himself in this life must choose, must love, what will perfect him. But it should be remembered that love ultimately issues in knowledge, the beatific vision. Cf. Gerald F. Van Ackeren, "The Finality of the College Course in Sacred Doctrine in the Light of the Finality of Theology," a paper read at the second annual meeting of Society of Catholic College Teachers of Sacred Doctrine, University of Notre Dame, 1956.

6 There is no absolute distinction between knowledge and its state of possession, as if a knowledge of one sort could not function as a condition of possession for another knowledge. As we shall see, the knowledge of faith is an existential condition of the possession of any other knowledge in a Catholic college.

CHAPTER 4

1 Absurdity begins when one thinks there is a way of knowing entirely independent of the object known. One might then talk about learning the scientific method without studying any scientific facts. There is no way of knowing that is not a way of knowing certain kinds of data. But about the same data there are better and more accurate ways of knowing, depending on the student's maturity and experience in considering such data.

2 *Summa Theologiae*, I, q. 85, a. 3 (*Basic Writings of St. Thomas*, trans. Anton C. Pegis [New York: Random House, 1944], I, 818-21).

3 This division, in its general sweep, is taken from George P. Klubertanz, S.J., *Introduction to the Philosophy of Being* (New York: Appleton-Century-Crofts, 1952), pp. 1-4, 258-86. Also see Aristotle, *Posterior Analytics*, II, 19, 99b15-100b15 (*Basic Works of Aristotle*, ed. Richard McKeon [New York: Random House, 1941], p. 185); Yves Simon, *Traité du libre arbitre* (Liège: Sciences et Lettres, 1951), pp. 31-66.

4 "It is like a rout in battle stopped by first one man making a stand and then another, until the original formation has been restored" (Aristotle, *Posterior Analytics*, II, 19, 100a10-100a14 [*Basic Works of Aristotle*, p. 185]).

5 Another example, less technical, is seen in this proposition: "The size of any snake can be measured accurately." A man, relying on spontaneous knowledge, would be inclined to affirm that proposition. Here is what a scientist has to say: "A basic obstacle in studying size in snakes is the difficulty of measuring them or of accurately estimating

their length. The long, attenuated body can shorten considerably by means of a few insignificant kinks. It is virtually impossible to straighten out a large snake all at one time. . . . The coiled snake can be unrolled carefully along a ruler or tape measure to get its length, but slips and errors are a common hazard. Another method is to lay a string or soft wire along the back, carefully following each coil or twist of the body, and then measure the length of string required. When used with care and some practice these methods can be employed on dead or preserved snakes to give fairly accurate results, but sometimes even two scientists will not get identical measurements for the same individual. . . . The measuring of live snakes is even more difficult. The snake is constantly contracting part of its body, and there is danger of stretching the animal too much or of not getting all the kinks out. A few techniques have been devised for measuring smaller live specimens, but I know of no really practical method for accurately measuring a live snake more than 15 feet in length. . . . Dealing with skins is misleading in the extreme. Carefully conducted experiments show that you simply can't get the skin off the snake without stretching it" (James A. Oliver, *Snakes in Fact and Fiction* [New York: Macmillan, 1958], pp. 19-20).

6 These are also the tools of artistic literary knowledge. The difference between artistic and reflective elaborated knowledge is not in the tools used but in what one does—construct or analyze—with such tools.

7 Jacques Maritain, in "Thomist Views on Education" (*Modern Philosophies and Education*, 54th Yearbook, Part I, National Society for the Study of Education [Chicago: University of Chicago Press, 1955], pp. 57-90), calls such knowledge a perfection of "natural intelligence." Here "natural" is not opposed either to unnatural or to supernatural but to "trained to specialization." Scientific knowledge would be specialized knowledge.

8 *Works of William Paley, D.D.* (London: Nelson and Sons, 1855). For his argument, see pp. 436-546.

9 The reader should look closely at the meaning given "scientific knowledge." Commonly today *science* means "the natural sciences," which proceed by the experimental method, and *scientific* would be an adjectival form of "natural science." As used here "scientific knowledge" is not limited to natural sciences. The term applies to any knowledge that gives reasons (or causes) to ground certain and sure knowledge. When I wish to refer to knowledge that proceeds experimentally, I shall use the term "natural science." This usage is not arbitrary. Aside from the fact that the division of knowledge needs such a term, the history of Western thought before 1600 justifies it.

10 Some knowledge, the speculative sciences, do not partialize; but this is owing to the fact that they are, besides being sciences, also wisdom. That is, they deal with all that is, even though they deal only

with one aspect of all things. Thus metaphysics deals with the one aspect of the existence of whatever is. Now, existence is so central and pervasive that instead of partializing knowledge it broadens metaphysics to include everything except nothing. The same is true of theology because all things are related to God as their source and end. As knowledge they are limited to their own viewpoints and thereby differ from other knowledge such as physics, economics, anatomy. But the viewpoints of metaphysics and theology do not constrict their consideration to just one sort of being or to one aspect of some beings but open their interest to everything that is or can be, though still from one viewpoint. To see how this applies to theology, see Etienne Gilson, *Elements of Christian Philosophy* (New York: Doubleday and Company, 1960), pp. 22-42.

11 Suppose that a student did not know that "what is cannot simultaneously not be." The teacher could appeal to no facts, since a fact could just as well be a nonfact at the moment of appeal. That is, the paper in this book would be both white and not white, as well as being paper and not paper, and would not be while it was. With no facts to appeal to, what has the student mind to assent to? If there is no possibility of a student assent, there is no possibility of teaching either. In short, without an understanding, implicit or explicit, of the principle of noncontradiction learning is impossible.

12 It is not necessary to go into which arts the liberal arts college should teach. In the later Middle Ages the "liberal arts" were seven: grammar, logic, rhetoric, arithmetic, geometry, astronomy, and music. In general these were the knowledges that made it possible for a man of that day to learn whatever he wanted to learn. In this sense they were liberating. The American liberal arts college has added most of the fine arts, at least for purposes of appreciation. The fine arts studied with the view to production gravitate towards professional schools rather than departments in liberal arts colleges, no matter how they may happen to be named. But to go into the question of what arts belong in a liberal arts college is to start another book.

13 We can know "nothing" when we make it a denial of being, where it is a relative nothing. That is, we consider it as a denial of being. We can say, for instance, "Nothing is not knowable."

14 Gerard Smith, S.J., "The Knowledge of Man" (unpublished faculty lecture, Marquette University).

15 The following acts of knowledge necessarily deal with private facts: sensation, prudential judgments, aesthetic judgments. Acts of sensation deal only with what exists here and now in these singular circumstances. Prudential judgments determine what is best for me to do here and now in these present circumstances. Thus besides dealing with private, here-and-now facts, they also deal privately with these, seeing that my personal history partly determines the best for me.

Aesthetic judgments are dependent partly on the capacity of the judger to appreciate the artistic excellence of the product of art.

16 This and the next sixteen paragraphs were originally published in an article, "Causality in the Classroom," *Modern Schoolman*, XXVII (1951), 138-46. Permission to use this material has kindly been granted by the editor.

17 The answer given here owes more than inspiration to St. Thomas Aquinas. See his *Truth*, trans. Robert W. Mulligan, S.J., and Others (3 vols. Chicago: Henry Regnery Company, 1952-1954), II, 139-45.

18 Plato, *Meno*, 86. Plato is talking of certain knowledge, not of right opinion. In the *Republic*, Bk. VI, education is defined as turning to the light of the Ideas and the Good (*Dialogues of Plato*, trans. Benjamin Jowett [New York: Random House, 1937], I, 366).

19 Plato, *Meno*, 82-85 (*ibid.*, I, 361-65).

20 John Dewey, *Democracy and Education* (New York: Macmillan, 1926), p. 31. Cf. p. 74, where he says that we do not refine original impulse activity but select the response most useful in the face of a definite stimulus and coordinate the different factors of the response which takes place.

21 See Avicenna, *De Anima*, Pars V, c. 5.

22 Plato, *Meno*, 80 (Jowett, I, 360).

23 The teacher's signs are primarily words, though gestures and inflections help.

24 For the philosophy of the sign see *The Material Logic of John of St. Thomas: Basic Treatises*, trans. Yves R. Simon, John J. Glanville, G. Donald Hollenhorst (Chicago: University of Chicago Press, 1955), pp. 388-404.

25 To say that purely personal facts cannot be taught may seem strange to one who realizes that teaching is itself an art and therefore highly personal. So it is. But the art of teaching is not an art that works on the facts. The art of teaching works on the means of presenting facts. The teacher uses the art of grammar, logic, and rhetoric to order his means—words, actions, gestures—of presenting to the student's mind the facts present to his mind. The teacher's art is therefore highly personal. When his art works not on the means of presentation but on the facts being taught, he ceases to be a teacher and becomes a deceiver.

26 Mass-produced products are not strictly art-made but machine-made. The spot at which art enters such production is the action of designing, which is a matter of personal vision. After that each product is fully caused by, and therefore foreseeable in, its die.

27 There is no exception to this. Sacred theology is specified by its facts, even though the "fact" here is what God has told us. In other knowledge the facts may be supplied by the word of other men. In some

knowledge the facts are the things which come into our own immediate experience.

28 For a critical example, see the way in which Robert J. Henle, S.J., discovers the existential act in sense experience (*Method in Metaphysics* [Milwaukee: Marquette University Press, 1951], pp. 1-73).

29 R. G. Collingwood (*An Essay on Metaphysics* [Oxford: Clarendon Press, 1940], p. 14) concludes that there is no metaphysics because there are no facts for it to be about.

CHAPTER 5

1 There is another class of moral influences, morally related knowledges. This would include religious knowledge (the faith), ethics, and in general those knowledges that include knowledge of their good use, a class of knowledge we shall have occasion to explain later in this chapter. Since this class of knowledge will receive full attention in Chapter 6, I have decided not to consider it here as setting up moral conditions for other knowledges. Strictly speaking, ethics is a knowledge that sets the existential conditions for other knowledges and for itself as well. This point will be made clear in Chapter 7.

2 *Ethics*, I, 4, 109b1-10. See the *Basic Works of Aristotle*, ed. R. McKeon (New York: Random House, 1941), pp. 937-38.

3 For a full and technical discussion of the role of sense powers in human knowing, see George P. Klubertanz, S.J., *The Discursive Power* (St. Louis: Modern Schoolman, 1952).

4 What is said here applies to a teacher, not to a research economist. The man capable of economic research may or may not bring in non-economic aspects to suit his own purposes. As teacher, he must always be aware of how his words and actions influence the student. One such effect is noted in the next paragraph of the text.

5 Perhaps the example used above seems weighted in favor of the point being made. It is, or else it would be of little help in seeing the point. Other equivalent learning situations for a Catholic are to learn about man and nature with no mention of God, to learn about civil law with no mention of the natural law, to learn about marriage with no mention of the sacrament, to learn ethics with no mention of the life of supernatural grace. The test case is mathematics. Even mathematics one has learned needs to be related to other knowledges, especially in our day when some thinkers, using symbolic logic, have tried to reduce all knowledge to a mathematical type—a position that leaves faith outside the pale of knowledge.

6 Marjorie Reeves (*Three Questions in Higher Education* [New Haven: Hazen Foundation, 1955]) argues that this is from time to time the duty of the teacher. This booklet cannot be recommended too highly for its profound insights into the teacher-student relation.

7 I have not taken the case where respect for the teacher works on the emotions of the student in such a way that the student accepts whatever the teacher says because he likes the teacher. Such "liking" is no aid to understanding but rather a handicap. Personable teachers must watch lest this kind of personal influence make student thinking more difficult. To sway an audience by emotional appeal is no less a temptation to a competent teacher than to a political orator.

8 The Catholic faith can be described as a creed, a cult, and a code. But the proper order should be kept. For the creed grounds both the cult and the code, not the other way round, as if either cult or code grounded the creed. When there is question of anyone's learning by making assents, the major part of the faith is creed, a lesser part of it is code and cult.

9 See T. Lincoln Bouscaren, S.J., and Adam C. Ellis, S.J., *Canon Law, A Text and Commentary* (3rd ed.; Milwaukee: Bruce Publishing Company, 1957), pp. 766-69.

10 The Index of Prohibited Books (Vatican: Polyglot Press, 1948). For a brief explanation of the Catholic position on reading and censorship of prohibited books see R. A. Burke, *What Is the Index?* (Milwaukee: Bruce Publishing Company, 1952).

11 See the *Descriptive List of Professional and Nonprofessional Duties in Libraries* (Chicago: American Library Association, 1948), p. 61.

12 *Areopagitica, Prose Works of John Milton*, ed. St. John (London: Bahn, 1848), II, 97.

13 It is not likely that the Church and the American Library Association will agree on what is clearly harmful. At least on matters of heresy, it is hard to see how anyone besides God or His representative would have anything to say that is significant, either negatively or positively.

14 Readers familiar with theological discussions of the relation of faith to reason will recognize the famous "negative norm" theory; that is, that the faith is a negative norm for reason, informing reason what it cannot hold. The terminology is not too felicitous, since it calls up the image of babies who need a sitter to keep them from tearing up the house. Moreover, this role, no matter how stated, is not peculiar to the faith. Any and every truth can do the same for reason, since it is merely the application of the principle of noncontradiction. Hence I have given this relation of faith to learning the minor place it deserves. Also, I have shifted the terminology from the negative role of repression to the positive role of purification.

15 For a philosophical explanation of this possibility see George P. Klubertanz, S.J., *The Philosophy of Human Nature* (New York: Appleton-Century-Crofts, 1953), pp. 412-27.

16 *How We Think* (New York: D. C. Heath and Company, 1910), p. 154. Dewey makes his scientific method exceedingly general. But he

does exclude knowledge grounded on the authority of man and God. This excludes faith from the category of valid knowledge.

17 The context of our consideration requires that the reason against intellectual imperialism be derived from the faith. In another context, and one perhaps more thorough, one could start from the nature of scientific knowledge. In discussing such knowledge in Chapter 4, we indicated its necessary specialization, consisting of purifying data, developing special reasoning methods suitable to this precise data, and constructing a special terminology to handle the generated conclusions. This line of consideration would lead one to see that any single highly developed scientific method would become progressively more adapted to a progressively more limited field of data. The proliferation of natural sciences pretty well justifies this analysis of science. If a fisherman makes his net to catch just one size fish, he can hope to succeed in catching this one size. The ones he does not surround or the ones that slip through his net do not thereby cease to be fish.

18 The best of classical Greece and Rome was not good enough to meet the needs of man. See Charles N. Cochrane, *Christianity and Classical Culture* (Oxford: Clarendon Press, 1939).

19 A. P. D'Entrèves (*Natural Law* [London: Hutchinson House, 1951], pp. 48-64) shows the rationalism that underlies both the American and French Declarations.

20 Etienne Gilson, "Science, Philosophy and Religious Wisdom," *A Gilson Reader*, ed. A. C. Pegis (New York: Doubleday and Company, 1957), p. 215.

21 This distinction between good knowledge and the good use of knowledge is taken from Gerard Smith, S.J., *The Truth That Frees* (Milwaukee: Marquette University Press, 1956), pp. 28-56.

22 Sociology and economics could be placed in this category were it not for the fact that the contemporary progress of these sciences has been produced by a method imitating the natural sciences, in which moral factors are studiously excluded. The arts of grammar, logic, and rhetoric share in morally related knowledge because they are the disciplines that are most useful in attaining this knowledge.

23 No one term will name the class of knowledge under consideration. "Moralistic" would exclude all except ethics and moral theology. "Humanities," originally applied to the ancient classics and belles-lettres, now stands for what is not a natural or a social science. "Liberal" is sometimes used as a substitute for humanities, but this usage flies in the face of history. Since no single name is satisfactory, it seems preferable just to keep repeating phrases, awkward as this may be.

24 *Apology, Dialogues of Plato*, trans. Jowett (New York: Random House, 1937), I, 423.

25 Francis Bacon, *Novum Organum*, LXXXI, *English Philosophers from Bacon to Mill*, ed. E. A. Burtt (New York: Modern Library, 1938), p. 56.
26 Descartes, *Discourse on Method*, Part VI, *The Philosophy of Descartes*, trans. J. Veitch (New York: Tudor Publishing Company), p. 192.
27 Erwin Schrödinger, *Science and Humanism* (London: Cambridge University Press, 1951), p. 4.
28 John Henry Cardinal Newman, *Apologia pro Vita Sua* (New York: Modern Library, 1950), Part VII, p. 242.
29 Kenneth E. Boulding, "Economics," *Religious Perspectives in College Teaching*, Hoxie N. Fairchild and Others (New York: Ronald Press, 1952), p. 375.

CHAPTER 6

1 One science, metaphysics, can take man out of self and this world. But metaphysics has come upon such hard days in the last two centuries that it can do little more at present than fight for its life in American colleges.
2 Once he knows what is, he can consider this thing as prior to its actual existence here and now and thereby know what can be. We shall drop the "can be" from the rest of our analysis, because it is a derivative knowledge from knowledge of what is.
3 *Opticks*, Book I, Prop. X, Prob. V (New York: Dover, 1952), p. 179.
4 If a mind happened upon one red apple, it would also know that it was not itself red apple. But this part of the example can be overlooked in the present explanation.
5 This mystery is not one that physics tries to explain; but it is still present in the data, and it is present in the data after its physical explanation is completed.
6 One can, of course, bypass the mysterious in such data by refusing to consider any aspect of the data that cannot be made definite by measurement, a perfectly legitimate process up to a point. That point is reached when one thinks he has explained all the data, whereas he has merely dissolved mystery by decree.

   In the facts of experience we never succeed in identifying structure and the structured, or cause and effect. Mystery resides in both spots. At its peak, mystery resides in the impossibility of identifying structure and cause. If this identification would be made, there would be no mystery left in the data of our experience.
7 See Kenneth E. Boulding: "It is also true, however, that it is possible to retreat into abstractions from the demands which the real world is making upon us, and to take refuge from the demands of the moral law behind a screen of scientific indifference. The prolonged contemplation of abstract systems may also lead to a certain cynicism and

weariness: a paralysis of the will-to-good sets in because of a sense of the immense complexity of social life and the ill effects of a rash do-good-ism. It was not the economists who liberated slaves or who passed the Factory Acts, but the rash and ignorant Christians" ("Economics," *Religious Perspectives in College Teaching,* Hoxie N. Fairchild and Others [New York: Ronald Press, 1952], p. 376).

8 *Philosophy and Politics,* "National Book League Fourth Annual Lecture" (London: Cambridge University Press, 1947), pp. 24-25.

9 *Dogmatism and Tolerance* (New Brunswick: Rutgers University Press, 1952), pp. 11-12.

10 This·is the name of an article by Harold C. Hunt in *School Executive,* LXXI (May 1952), 19-22.

11 *Life,* Dec. 1, 1952, p. 36. The editorial is a comment on the annual statement of the American Catholic hierarchy on religion in America and the response of other groups to the statement.

12 Hollis L. Casswell, "Are the Public Schools Irreligious?" *Teachers College Record,* LIV (April 1953), 357-65. (Italics his.)

13 The Presbyterians state this position firmly: "We believe that a 'common core' or residuum of religious belief agreeable to all faiths as a basis for teaching is insufficient and misleading; that religious commitment arises in a specific and concrete religious community, highly articulate, and never abstracted into common elements . . . While we neither expect nor desire any teacher to indoctrinate any form of sectarianism, neither do we countenance the teaching of devitalized 'common faith' as a proper substitute for highly specific religious belief" (*The Church and the Public Schools,* An Official Statement of 169th General Assembly of the Presbyterian Church in U.S.A. [Philadelphia: Board of Christian Education of the Presbyterian Church in the U.S.A., 1957], p. 13).

14 Harry E. Fosdick makes this same point about university teaching: "Some seem to think that neutrality toward religion requires that we leave religion out of the university, forget it, omit it, arrange our curricula as though religion did not exist. But look at a university which does that! Is it being neutral? Is it not rather teaching something very definite: namely, that it is omitable, dispensable, negligible?" ("The Most Critical Problem in Our American Universities," *Modern Education and Human Values* [Pittsburgh: University of Pittsburgh Press, 1954], V, 38-39).

15 *The Church and the Public Schools,* p. 9.

16 Casswell, "Are the Public Schools Irreligious?" p. 385.

17 *Moral and Spiritual Values in the Public Schools,* Report of Educational Policies Commission of National Education Association and the American Association of School Administrators, 1951, p. 78. This report is the father of all statements on the moral and spiritual values in public schools.

18 An example is that of Dewey's position—considered in Chapter 5—that all valid knowledge must be acquired by a method similar to that used in the natural sciences.

19 *Idea of a University*, ed. C. F. Harrold (New York: Longmans, Green and Company, 1947), p. xxxiv.

20 The two faiths differ considerably in other respects. The word of a man might conceivably not be trustworthy; the word of God could never be. Again, what one learns from a man, he could conceivably learn for himself, excepting of course historical facts caught up in time; the divine mysteries cannot be known by man's unaided natural powers. Again, faith in another man's word begins with the decision to honor his word; divine faith begins with God, not man—"No one can come to me unless he is enabled to do so by my Father" (John 6:66). Finally, the word of another man may witness to the truth; the word of God both witnesses to the truth and binds the hearer to accept it.

21 *Modes of Being* (Carbondale, Ill.: Southern Illinois University Press, 1958), pp. 3-4.

22 Notice that the theological knowledge, though scientific, does not have the clarity of the human sciences, since its premises do not contain the evident and self-evident but what is known on the word of God. Thus the obscurity that attaches to the original premises is also present in the conclusions from these premises. And if this obscurity were never dissipated, theology would never be a science in the full sense. But the obscurity of the premises, and therefore also of the conclusions, will be dissipated when the divine mysteries are revealed directly to the human mind in the beatific vision. As Y. Simon points out (in an unpublished lecture, "The Rationality of the Christian Faith"), our theological knowledge in this life is very similar to that of beginning students of science who, still dependent "upon a teacher, are eagerly awaiting the time when they will be able to master the principles and do without witnesses; their work is scientific in substance and tends toward the state of science."

23 One characteristic of such a mind is its readiness to find bad will in all who disagree. This cast of mind is not surprising in one that attains its certainly mainly by will. If anyone disagrees, it must be owing to his bad will.

24 This seems to be what Milton Mayer had in mind as the best that Church-related schools could do. He says: "To the extent that they [denominational institutions] nourish the vestige of God, which they alone now harbor, they will, I think, progressively lose their status as educational institutions. Since they are now handicapped, they might as well go whole hog" ("The Vestige of God," *Commonweal*, 52 [Education Issue, April 14, 1950], 14).

CHAPTER 7

1 At this point I am no longer reporting the opinion of others.

2 In most discussions, motives are considered in some propositional form, such as "I prefer to be honest." But this is only a knowledge transcription of the act of telling the truth. It is clearer, because closer to the facts, to refer to the motive as that which moves (attracts) me to desire it.

3 In Chapter 3 we had occasion to consider free choice—the young man deciding to marry—as that which perfects a man fully. Here the point to be made is the difference between value and motive. The nature of free choice is sufficiently important to stand repetition from a new angle. If this proves to be boring, the reader of course has ways of protecting himself.

4 Noël Mailloux, O.P., develops this point about free actions. "Free activity, corresponding to the most perfect activity to which man is capable, is certainly the activity in which least is left to indeterminacy and unpredictability. In other words, such behavior is fully controlled precisely because it is fully determined, because it constitutes the most adequate and accurate answer one can give to the more or less complicated set of demands imposed by reality at a given moment. It is easy to see that the more one has developed some skill and can master a situation, the more he takes account of even the minutest details. Each aspect of his activity corresponds to a definite element of reality, and finds in it its ultimate determination. The more complex the situation to which we have to adapt, the more necessary it is to surpass the gross and rigid determination achieved through mechanization or automatization. The extremely precise adaptability of the artist, of the craftsman, of the professional player, requires nothing less than the plasticity of free determination—free because it has to be complete.

"But as free determination implies self-determination, what we call free activity is nothing else than self-determined activity." Cf. "Psychic Determinism, Freedom and Personality," *The Human Person*, ed. M. B. Arnold and J. A. Gasson, S.J. (New York: Ronald Press, 1954), p. 273.

5 Elizabeth G. Salmon makes this point in a metaphysical setting in *The Good in Existential Metaphysics* (Milwaukee: Marquette University Press, 1953), p. 24.

6 If needs are considered in a general way, say, the need for food in general, they are obviously common to all men. But such general needs are not properly the object of choices, since no one can choose to eat food in general. The framework of our present discussion demands values that can be motives for choices.

7 See Chapter 5, pp. 140-41.

8 Christopher F. Mooney, S.J. ("College Theology and Liberal Education," *Thought*, XXXIV [Autumn 1959], 325-46) adds the doctrine of the Trinity to show that self-giving is the proper perfection of persons.

9 Johann Lindworsky, S.J. (*The Training of the Will*, trans. from the German by A. Steiner and E. A. Fitzpatrick [Milwaukee: Bruce Publishing Company, 1929]) makes a unified life ideal the most critical knowledge-factor in good moral choices.

CHAPTER 8

1 I cannot refrain from quoting the cynical remark of the coach of a losing football team: "We are training the boys to virtue this year." Like the unsuccessful coach, college teachers not concentrating on knowledge can always say that they are training to virtue. The problem becomes more serious when the teachers are not cynical.

moral, 8, 186-213, 217-18
morally good, 195, 197-98
motives and values in, 190-93, 199-200
nature of, 45-47, 188-200
preferential knowledge included, 199-200
role of in perfection of man, 45-47, 48-49, 187-88, 218
specification of by knowledge, 131-32, 188, 198-202,
    223-24, 225
speculative knowledge and, 47-49, 187-88
See also Moral choices
Christ
as redeemer, 128, 206
divinity of, 180-81
God and man, 182, 207, 208
knowledge of presented by theology, 182, 206-08
life of, 207, 209
Christian liberal arts college, 5, 20-24, 185, 226-27.
    See also Catholic liberal arts college
Christian perfection, 20-22
Church, education and, 5, 114-22, 131-32, 137-38, 205-09,
    227-28
Cicero, 3
Cochrane, Charles H., 238
Code of Canon Law, 117
College
Catholic, 2-4, 5-7, 8, 11-30, 52-53, 89-90, 97-148, 150-51,
    184-85, 204-11, 215-28
church-related, 20-24, 27, 185, 226-27
founders of, 23-24, 70
nonchurch-related, 5-6, 184-85
objectives of, 2-4, 8, 11-30, 174-75, 215-16, 225-28
secular, 6, 184-85

Subject matter
anti-intellectualism resulting from neglect of, 171-85
destruction of scientific ideals through neglect of, 175
extrinsic reasons for assent permitted by neglect of,
172-74
in Catholic colleges, 131-32, 184-85
intellectual drive blocked by neglect of, 171-76
moral implications of, 102-03, 106-07
necessity of balance between faith and, 184-85
neglect of through overemphasis on existential conditions, 172-84
neglect of through overemphasis on faith, 176-84
neglect of when good will is substituted for intellectual
discipline, 173-76
overemphasis on in secular colleges, 184-85
overemphasis on resulting from demand that all knowledge exhibit character of scientific knowledge, 161-66
overemphasis on through neglect of faith, 150-71
partial skepticism resulting from overemphasis on, 151-
61, 170
presentation of as existential condition of student
assents, 101, 102-08, 153-57, 168-71
relation of to existential conditions of assent, 149-85
teachability of, 93, 104, 209
teacher's knowledge of, 101
uncontrolled existential conditions resulting from overemphasis on, 166-70

Taylor, H. O., 229
Teacher
as giver of knowledge, 76-79, 82-84
examples used by, 104-05, 108, 209

About this book

Teaching and Morality was designed by William Nicoll of EDIT, INC.
It was set in the composing room of LOYOLA UNIVERSITY PRESS. The text
is 11 on 14 Caledonia; the notes 8 on 10.

It was printed by PHOTOPRESS, INC., on WARREN's 60-pound English
Finish paper and bound by A. C. ENGDAHL AND COMPANY, INC.